How To Succeed Without Really Winning

Also by George Huitker

Poetry

An Unfamiliar Sea
The Actor Is Happy
An Unfamiliar Actor

Prose

Not Just Footy
Little Life

How To Succeed Without Really Winning

Not Just Footy II

George Huitker

How To Succeed Without Really Winning
ISBN 978 1 74027 309 1
Copyright © George Huitker 2005

First published 2005
Reprinted 2014, 2015

GINNINDERRA PRESS
PO Box 3461 Port Adelaide 5015
www.ginninderrapress.com.au

Printed by Rainbow Press, Dry Creek, SA

Contents

Foreword		**9**
Part One	**Starting Eleven**	**17**
Training Module 1	Kaizen	19
Training Module 2	Life and Death Matters	28
Training Module 3	Clubbing	40
Training Module 4	Rage Against the Machine	52
Training Module 5	Dad vs Dad	58
Training Module 6	Leaving Jackals at the Gate	70
Training Module 7	Taking Penalties	79
Training Module 8	Bench Warming	91
Training Module 9	How I Learned to Stop	
	Worrying & Love the Bomb	101
Training Module 10	What Coach Is That?	111
Training Module 11	Old-fashioned Concepts	
	Like Allegiance & Loyalty	124
Part Two	**Match Reports**	**145**
12: Heads		147
13: Tails		193
Part Three	**Send-off Reports**	**249**
14: Loreto		251
15: How To Succeed Without Winning		262
16: Bibliography		267
17: Acknowledgements		274
About the Author		276

For Patrick Britten,
Walter Learning
and John Leyshon

And all those coaches who give their time, voluntarily,
to nurture impressionable if not volatile young souls
instead of having a quiet afternoon at home.

Winning never lifts him as high as losing drags him down.

Gunther Bosch, Boris Becker's coach

*

Some people think there's no place for sentiment in football – there is now.

George Banks, *Banksie*, 2002

*

While it's important to have balance in your life, it takes a certain obsessiveness to be outstanding.

Ric Charlesworth, *Inside Sport*, July 2003

Foreword

I'm going to be honest. The title confused me.

I first came across *How To Succeed Without Really Winning* when I was fourteen. George Huitker was, among other things, my drama teacher, soccer coach, chief Freddo Frog supplier and out-of-hours musical education officer. I was, among other things, intent on one day playing cricket for Australia. As I was accustomed to consuming sports titles such as *The Winner's Bible*, *The Making of Champions* and *Win Or No One Will Love You*,* George's title piqued my curiosity but also some schoolboy scepticism.

Like many of my adolescent friends who feature in this book, I had been indoctrinated with the notion that sport is about winning trophies, being selected for rep teams, becoming a national hero, and maybe one day appearing in a fast-food commercial (that teaches other kids to believe the same). To win is to succeed, right?

Thankfully, George Huitker believes in a different story.

* Okay, I made that last one up.

I first met 'H' as a twelve-year-old at the try-outs for the 2003 Radford College U15 Bill Turner Cup team. Despite the fact that I was half the size of everyone else, H selected me in the team. We won a tight penalty shoot-out (the only one of H's teams ever to win one – see Training Module 7), lost the cup, but succeeded in laying the foundations for a wonderful coach-player, teacher-student, human-human relationship.

As a young player, I was struck by H's colourful sense of humour, ability to make every individual feel valuable (even a skinny twelve-year-old bench warmer), and rare knack of making you work hard and enjoy yourself simultaneously. Playing under H we gradually learned an approach to sport that is far removed from the 'silly, stupid, serious systems' of politics, pressure and collective neuroses in junior sport that are so entertainingly depicted in this book. Our soccer experience was characterised by enjoyment, challenge, creativity, (dare I say) love, and a healthy dose of the ridiculous.

By the time my Radford soccer team reached the U18 ACT Premier division, our team had developed a unique warm-up routine. While the opposition sides dutifully sidestepped between ladders and cones, we were headering imaginary balls with Mario Kart sound effects, practising our 'stretchican wave' of choreographed stretching, then getting in the zone with 'Ain't No Mountain High Enough' by Marvin Gaye and Tammi Terrell pumping in the change rooms. Those who have read this book will know it's not really important that we performed very well on the pitch that year, with this warm-up routine and H at the helm. Yet, interestingly, it's true.

Since graduating from Radford College seven years ago, I have become a professional cricket player, firstly with the Victorian Bushrangers and now with the NSW Blues and the Sydney Sixers. Being surrounded by sport, I am certainly familiar with all the species of coach described in George's frighteningly accurate 'Beginner's Guide to Identifying Coaches in Your Own Backyard' (see Training Module 10). I have seen the Pacers, the Statisticians, the Drill Sergeants, the Optimists, the Al Pacinos, the Parent/Coaches, the Screamers and the Cockatoos.

Yet, despite our close relationship, I find George very difficult to categorise, as a person and a coach. He is a teacher, a friend, a poet, a philosopher. He is fanatical yet detached, bold yet vulnerable, sincere yet ironic. He has a child's sight and a sage's vision. A fine passage in this book describes a type of coach, the Saint, as

> Someone whose little sayings or small but significant gestures lift off from the paddocks of the past and stay with you for a lifetime. Someone who shows

you ways of making the struggle in small things like sport, and shows that larger things, like life, are well worth working at.

While the George Huitker is definitely its own species of coach, this trait he shares with the Saint. Through charming and humorous stories of his coaching adventures, in this book George guides us through the landscape of junior sport. We meet murderous parents, heartbreaking penalties, deified defensive formations and 'peas on a conveyor belt' academies, but also lovable characters, comedic bungles, rousing speeches and improbable triumphs.

George frequently refers to the Japanese principle of kaizen – continual improvement – and encourages us to look 'behind the result'. Indeed, it is in looking behind the stories of struggle, insecurity, ingenuity and occasional heroism that we find the book's most valuable message. Sport is about affirming life, not trying to change it. It is about enjoyment, learning and becoming better equipped to handle future challenges on and off the field. H laments that people approach junior sport as if there is so much at stake in the result. Yet there is a lot at stake, just not in the conventional sense of winning and losing. Through sport we become acquainted with many of the nobler and baser expressions of humanity, and learn how we want to stand in relation to them.

In one beautiful passage, George describes watching a young Italian boy juggling a soccer ball between the arcades of the Palazzo Apostolico. He witnesses the boy's unadulterated joy as he loses himself in the dance of ball and body. George recognises the dual truth that this scene captures the pure essence of play for the sake of play, but is also linked to something important about what it takes to become world-class. In my cricketing career I have been fortunate to play with and against many of the best players in the world. I have learned that the tense, over-drilled, academy types that George describes as always looking constipated are often slow to truly flourish. Those who prevail at the top level seem to maintain something akin to the little bambino juggling for joy, despite the elevated pressure and consequences. Rahul Dravid, one of the greatest Indian batsmen of all time, described it as 'taking the spirit of the amateur – of discovery, of learning, of pure joy – into our profession'.* Also, adopting a kaizen philosophy may not only grant us a happier and healthier relationship with sport, it may help young players of all abilities to unlock their potential.

How To Succeed Without Really Winning portrays coaching as more of an art than a science. Indeed, many of the most enjoyable sections and useful insights arise from George's willingness to convey his vulnerability as a

* http://www.cricket.com.au/video/rahul-dravid-bradman-oration/2011-12-14

coach. It is not only players who must adopt an attitude of continual improvement: coaches must stumble their way to success as well. He experiences conflicting urges to yell at players for being crybabies, hide under the 'security blanket' of intricate whiteboard game plans, and maintain his dedicated 'nice guy' approach. Making the right call at the right moment involves trust and intuition as much as strategic prowess.

Much of the value of this book lies in its determination to keep sport in perspective. Most powerfully, George advocates that sporting teams should engage in acts of service to others. As well as helping those in need, team-based charity work can foster friendship, teamwork and gratitude, while keeping the sporting world from growing bigger and uglier than it needs to be. George has a phrase for it: unclogging one's humanity.

In my Radford days, I was lucky to be part of the first year of H's teamSUPPORT program. Under his tutelage, a group of my sports-loving peers organised sports activity afternoons for students from Black Mountain and Woden Schools with physical or intellectual disabilities. In later years the program has expanded to include visits to local nursing homes and time spent with indigenous communities in rural NSW.

The teamSUPPORT program had a strong influence on me, and certainly helped me to keep my own life and sporting dreams in perspective. In 2013, I founded a charity fundraising campaign called Batting for Change (www.battingforchange.com.au). We invite cricket lovers around Australia to donate a small amount of money for every six the Sydney Sixers hit in the Big Bash League to support the education of young men and women living in poverty around the cricket-playing world. In two years we have raised enough money for the LBW Trust charity to build three new classrooms at the Heartland School in Kathmandu, Nepal, and subsidise the tertiary education of 500 young women from Mumbai, India. I am excited to know that the actions of sportspeople can make a difference in the lives of those who need it most, and inspire others to do the same.

I am grateful that George has shared his delightful sporting stories in a book full of entertaining commentary laced with humour and irony, but I am most grateful that he is teaching us to look beyond winning and losing in sport, and find enjoyment in friendship, challenge, continual learning and the determination to help others.

There was a time when the title confused me. Now I'm confused as to why we aren't teaching every child about how to succeed without really winning – in sport and in life.

Ryan Carters
February 2015

Part One
Starting Eleven

Training Module 1
Kaizen

All hell's breakin' loose
Hey now people have you heard the news?
All hell's breakin' loose
Overloadin', blowin' my fuse

Kiss, *All Hell's Breakin' Loose*, 1983.

Americans go to psychiatrists more often than Italians
go to football matches, which is not easy to do! There's
got to be a lesson in there somewhere.

George Negus, *The World from Italy*, 2001

I think I lost it on the weekend.

I was screaming at the referee about a studs-up tackle
on my goalie which unfortunately resulted in the ball
being dislodged from his arms and unceremoniously
thwacked into the back of our net. Across the great divide,
opposition parents were mimicking my complaints to
the referee, some just hurling abuse, while another
parent actually entered the field of play to theatrically
pat the back of the goal-scorer – for the foul rather than

the goal – then waved sarcastically at me as he retreated back to the safety of his posse of rabid jackals.

I thought to myself, this is silly. We all really need to stop this for a minute, sit down together over a jasmine tea and think about why we're all getting so worked up about a junior sporting match. I read in *The Canberra Times* a report from the English Public Health Authority stating that

> ...on average, over a five-year period, the incidence of heart attack and stroke amongst male supporters increased by about 30 per cent when their local team lost a home match.

I really wouldn't wish a cardiac episode on anyone, not even opposition supporters.

Let's face it, all this negative energy disguised as barracking and loyalty is *unhealthy*. And while being dubiously motivated by it, I'm not convinced that in their hearts the kids playing the game appreciate it either. Then there's the poor referee, probably not all that much older than the participants, being blamed for everything from a bad offside call to third world famine.

All through the ensuing week, I decided to work out exactly what it is that drives us to such stupid acts of irresponsibility and immaturity during a sports match, especially when it's our kids who are playing. I picked up an old copy of *Inside Sport* (#138, July 2003), hoping for some answer within, and was pleasantly surprised to find, a few pages from the back, the accomplished former Australian women's hockey coach, Ric Charlesworth, postulating that sporting success was more about

> ...realising your potential, not what you achieve. It cannot simply be measured by whether you win or lose. You always need to look behind the result.

I figured, there's the rub. We are so conditioned to see success only in terms of winning that looking *behind* a performance is near impossible.

It is not helped when the media and our highly-paid sports heroes do such a fine job of suggesting that the dominate-at-all-costs mentality is the only way to fully experience success. I recall our Australian cricketers seeming outraged when the West Indies refused to lie down and die in the final test of the 2003 Caribbean tour. Or Lleyton Hewitt appearing to take personal umbrage at anybody challenging him to a close match on his way to the final of the 2005 Australian Open. Just think about what some of our more prominent and very successful sport stars actually propound when they smash their rackets, hurl their golf clubs, administer a muddy face massage or sneer at a batsman after nearly taking his head off. What they are saying is, *Winning to me is everything. I'm deserving of success and must not be challenged by impediments. If I can't get past an obstacle, I'm going to trash my equipment or try to grossly intimidate my opposition. I've worked far too hard not to be recognised, remembered and revered for being a winner. Maybe if I tantrum like a ten-year-old in front of a national audience, people will come to understand how important this is to me.*

What most forget is that without obstacles, opposition and adversity you have no sport.

American playwright David Mamet shrewdly noted in *Three Uses of the Knife* that

> …we rationalise, objectify and personalise the process of the game exactly as we do that of a play, a drama. For finally, it is a drama, with meaning for our lives. Why else would we watch it?

Mamet comes to the conclusion that we see our lives as a play in which we cast ourselves as the hero. So when we project ourselves as the central character in a sporting game (or transfer the hero status to a player or team), losing can feel like an unacceptable, if not personal failing. This is because heroes are not supposed to lose.

Often, a game assumes microcosmic proportions. It suckers us into believing that if we (or those we associate with) succeed on the sportsfield, this can transfer into success in our own lives. The television highlights assure us, winners are grinners. Wimbledon champion Boris Becker once recognised this in himself:

> When you are a young man, you are looking for your own identity, and winning is a way of expressing yourself. When I lost, I wanted to die. And because I thought in victory I became somebody, in defeat, it followed, I was nobody.

You can beat into the dirt any suggestion that you are a 'nobody' if you quite literally manage to do this to your opposition.

But as suggested, winning has its drawbacks. A top seed is well advised to enjoy the sensation of being Number 1 because fairly soon they're going to have to spend all their energy mulling over and working out how the blazes they're going to stay up there and negate an ever-growing fear of failure. As another former tennis hothead, John McEnroe once stated,

> People in the art business have a tendency to one day tell you you're the greatest artist that ever lived and the next second make you wonder if you'll ever sell a piece of art again. So I think I have a knowledge of that, because you have a fear when you go out on the court: fear of failure… I understand artists are needy and insecure.

Fellow 'artist' Joni Mitchell empathises with this fear of being unable to repeat success when she stated, 'Nobody ever asked Van Gogh to paint *A Starry Night* again – and again.' Winning is temporal and the sweet taste of success can stay an even shorter time in the mouth both on centre court and in the world of arty pursuits.

In his book *On Football*, Michael Parkinson warns us how careless we can become with our underpaid heroes of the past, allowing them to become ruthlessly sacked from the memory. He cites former English captain Danny Blanchflower's eloquent words on the temporal quality of success:

> In the highly intensive world of professional football the sun rises and sets with alarming suddenness. The world turns over every twenty-four hours, but not with the smooth astronomical rhythm that compels our planet. It just gives a quick, impulsive spin and the character who has been basking in the summit sunshine unexpectedly finds himself clinging desperately to the South Pole with cold, bare fingers.

It is a tough ask for any athlete to revisit those moments of bliss experienced at the loftier North Pole. Yet the athlete seems, more and more these days, only to be as good as his/her next championship with very little time to savour the previous victory. (Only a small percentage, like McEnroe, get to continue to have a regular, high-profile, expert voice in their chosen sports commentary boxes after putting away their broken rackets.) When sportsmen of Joe Di Maggio's pedigree say things like he did, after busting his guts in an exhibition baseball game, 'Well you never know – someone here might not have seen me before', you get some idea of how demanding and taxing it must be to be the best at something. And to continually need to prove it.

When you get used to winning and the associated accolades, you can forget how to lose. This is unfortunate, as losing is a part of life. It invariably happens to our reputations, hairlines, wallets, virginities, dreams, expectations, jobs, friendships, health and sometimes, tragically, to our loved ones.

Charlesworth speaks about a Japanese term *kaizen*, which essentially means 'continual improvement'. This notion is in stark contrast to the idea of 'continually proving yourself'. Maybe if success is seen more along the *kaizen*-line in both our lives and in sport, then the everyday realities of loss and self-doubt become infinitely more beatable. You can genuinely grow, develop and succeed through loss if you embrace *kaizen*. Surely then it is something we should instil a sense of in our kids.

We should stop living vicariously through them and allow them some unencumbered space in which to 'dance' on the sports paddocks every Saturday. What should also occur for us grown-ups is the realisation that impassioned rants at players, referees and coaches are nothing more than a statement of the ranter's own hopeless inadequacy: *I'm really not seeing much success in sport (or in my life) at the moment. I don't want to amount to nothing. So I demand that something goes right for me here and now because if it's going right for my son/daughter then it's definitely going right for me.*

One can only feel sympathy for these folk. As sport plays by its own rules and writes its own unpredictable script, winning is never any guarantee. So those of us who persist in the quest for global supremacy are pretty much heading for anything from mild disappointment to total despair. (Trace any despot. It all eventually falls apart.) Sadly, this ever-increasing number of sporting megalomaniacs usually take it all out on anyone but themselves. So when it's the kids on a playing field copping flak – as players or referees – we must have the courage to tell them to stop.

In redefining our attitude to success, we should leave the jackals at the gate. We can approach, more meaningfully and substantially, Charlesworth's 'culture of learning and humility' so absent on the cantankerous sidelines and training fields of junior, senior, amateur and professional sporting events. In short, seek development not domination. Then, almost ironically, you may well dominate in the long term. Ric Charlesworth's coaching CV will attest to this.

A friend of mine recently had the contents of his house removed by efficient thieves. However, he seemed genuinely unflustered by the theft and I remember asking him why that was. He replied that the thieves obviously needed his possessions more than he did. You have to admire that. In reframing his way of looking at the crime, he eliminated a great deal of anger, pain and regret which he might have otherwise unleashed on the cat, through a power tool, in a squash court or at a junior sporting event.

So I figured, the next time my team loses, I will not give a brass razoo about losing. I will accept that maybe the opposition needs the win more than I do. Then, my charges and I can get back to looking *behind* the result, past personal angst and anger, and seek out the real successes we may have overlooked had we not been so hip to this *kaizen* thing.

Training Module 2
Life and Death Matters

Life, it's bigger. It's bigger than you and you are not me.

REM, *Losing My Religion*, 1991.

Thankfully, sport can offer us more profound meaning and symbolic hope to offset the uglier aspects of our non-sporting reality.

On 7 June 2003, Jason McCartney's winning performance in his final AFL game in Kangaroo colours allowed us – and even the rival Tigers' supporters – to finally see, through a sporting context, some rays of light amidst the immeasurable dark cloud of the Bali tragedy. Dismayed by the injuries sustained during the bombings, McCartney considered giving away his football, but was talked out of it by his mother, Jan. God love her. As Kangaroos president Alan Aylett stated in the *Sydney Morning Herald*,

> That fleeting moment of self-doubt soon gave way to a new desire to fight back and now, less than a month later, he has reached his goal.

Wearing the numbers 88 and 202 on the front of his guernsey, in recognition of the number of Australians and the total number of people killed in the atrocity, McCartney ran out to play an uplifting game of monumental and highly symbolic significance. As described on the official Kangaroos' webpage:

> With the match in the balance – Richmond leading by three points in the dying minutes – the chance was there for the ultimate fairytale with McCartney positioned at full-forward. While he didn't kick the winning goal, he was instrumental in its creation. McCartney cleverly stopped the ball on the ground just outside his goal square, a slewed kick falling fortuitously into the path of Leigh Harding who made no mistake from point blank range. The goal put the team three points in front, with 28 minutes showing on the clock, a narrow lead they kept during the frantic final seconds with Richmond mounting an assault. The final siren saw an enormous outpouring of emotion by the Kangaroos towards their teammate. It was now the crowd's turn to watch McCartney, many no doubt with tears in their eyes, in awe of the journey he'd made.

This is sport at its best: a bunch of playing and non-playing people looking *behind* a result and recognising then celebrating through a game, the intrinsic value and potential of every single human life, providing us hope amidst the shadow of grave loss and significant despair.

McCartney retired after the game. Yet his one-match return was a significant symbol of hope and grit and rebirth and possibly even comfort to all who lost family and friends in Bali (and possibly at other times, in other ways). Within a month, Jason was back in the spotlight, having returned to Indonesia to attend and be a witness at the trial of Amrozi. He looked his would-be assassin square in the eye. I was reminded of Desmond Tutu's words: 'Look the beast in the eye. It has an uncanny habit of returning to hold us hostage.' I like to think that McCartney's willingness to confront not only the demon of self-doubt but this veritable demon of incomprehensible destruction (in the shape of a human), gave us all the courage to look our own beasts fairly and squarely in the eye. And scare them off a good long way so they need not return in a great big hurry.

McCartney's final match is reminiscent of a similarly uplifting soccer moment which occurred when Turkey defeated Northern Ireland 3–1 in Belfast in 1999. This victory occurred shortly after some devastating earthquakes rocked Turkey, leaving up to 15,000 dead. As *The Times* chief sports writer Rob Hughes reflected from London,

> Pride one can understand, but those reports spoke of some spiritual uplift, a sense of defiance and renewal from such a trivial event as a soccer match. From the

safe land on which I stand, that appears to invest too much in a sport...

As already indicated, people do go to great lengths to invest a great deal – maybe too much – into sporting games. Yet a well-timed achievement, such as the two outlined above by the Kangaroos and the Turks, can go a long way to commence some reparation of a fragile or tormented psyche...or country. Realistically, they cannot fully repair either the physical or mental rubble and debris caused by the more profound challenges of human existence. And as Hughes insinuates, there is only so much a sporting result can really do to heal the inconsolable hurt of those who have lost their loved ones in Bali or Turkey or even more recently in the devastating tsunami disaster. It is after all only a game, a diversion, a bandaid. But alternatively, none would deny that at moments such as these, as with powerful art, emotions can be stirred, inspired and rallied towards the road to healing, survival and transcendence. The World XI vs Asian XI cricket matches for the tsunami relief in early 2005 hopefully started the process of raising important funds and, more crucially, the spirits of the countries affected. I do not think this link between sport and charity is coincidental and I will explore it more fully in later chapters.

Unfortunately, for each positive symbolic slant taken from sport, an equally negative charge can be found to counter the argument, generally by just picking up the paper, watching the sporting highlights on television or attending a sports event where the stakes are far far far too high...

The steward suggested that we leave the stadium quickly, before they let the Cardiff supporters loose. 'It's a matter of life and death to some of them,' he explained to us gravely, pointing to the safety of the exits. This reminded me of something Liverpool manager Bill Shankly reputedly said, 'Some people think football is a matter of life and death – I can assure them it's more important than that.'

Well, to these away-supporters in this measly third round FA Cup clash against Coventry at Highfield Road in January 2003, football seemed to be as intense as anything I had ever experienced before. Had I the benefit of a crystal ball, I would have informed both sides of supporters that neither of the teams would get past round 4, so all the extreme anxiety was hardly worth a fig in the grand scheme of things. Let alone the violence. Not since playing my first match in goal with West Woden Under 8 Division 3 had I ever been so scared shitless at a football match. (I was relieved I had left my touring Under 16 Radford boys' and girls' sides with their billets in Derbyshire.)

On arrival, we somewhat stupidly disembarked near some arriving away-supporters' buses and directly in front of the stands set aside for Cardiff's travellers. My colleagues and I couldn't see the Welsh fans, but we could hear them, approaching rapidly, singing some bizarre Welsh war anthem filled with a plethora of consonants stuck in close succession and in which every third word was 'fckk'. I turned to friend and fellow coach Jann and suggested we run for our lives. Then this military truck screeched in front of the booth where I had picked up our tickets and a squadron of coppers in jackboots jumped out, brandishing bats and shields and looking like something out of *Black Hawk Down*. Surely this inconsequential football match was not the target for some terrorist attack?

The Welsh chanting was getting more deafening, threatening (and closer) so we decided it prudent not to stick around and see how the Coventry Security Services fared. We jogged rapidly around to the other side of Highfield Road where, to some relief, we managed to lose ourselves in a sky-blue sea of Coventry fans. The game started and all the rude Welsh chanting eventually (and considerably) quietened down after Coventry pumped in three goals, including a scorcher by Dean Holdsworth. I believe my players tried to spot me on Sky – I bought a garish sky-blue beanie for ease of identification – but alas, the cameramen seemed more interested in the action both on and mostly off the pitch.

In truth, I would have preferred that my charges hadn't seen the jackbooted coppers having a bit of biffo with some Cardiff nutters who were, ironically, being contained by a huge circle of security personnel post-match so that the Coventry supporters could get home safely, with no fights breaking out. I saw one guy, keen to get back to his home in Merthyr Tydfil, thrashing frenetically at a policeman equipped with a handy bat and shield who, without equivocation, would not let the Welshman pass. I remember thinking it was a good thing that all that pent-up aggression was not set loose to rampantly fly towards some nice, innocent people who were actually there *to watch football*, like the dad and his kid seated next to me. Incredibly, this man and his son seemed more than able to ignore the foul-mouthed ditties and antisocial post-match fisticuffs happening around them, all with considerable and commendable apathy as if it was all 'everyday'.

Not taking my players to this fixture was wise.

I recall walking past one of the tour buses as we exited the stadium. Someone had thrown a brick through a bus window. The driver was surveying the damage, shaking his head and muttering. He had this worn-out, frustrated look of acceptance as he reached for a broom. How could anyone make rational sense of this violence? In that *Inside Sport* article, Ric Charlesworth continued to say that

> ... sport is a discreet thing that people can throw their hearts into and be stimulated by. It's a life and culture that's not destructive – people don't die.

Yet I couldn't help but feeling that had the security guards been less effective at taming this frothing animal – which struggled furiously to be unmuzzled – somebody might well have.

That night on television I saw footage of the fans at the match, one of whom (from which team, I could not discern) was glaring straight into the camera in a way that would have given Hannibal the Cannibal the Hershey-squirts for a fortnight. There was nothing but sheer, unblinking aggression there and it seemed, disturbingly, to be the look of a man desperate to give expression to that anger – an anger which I am certain had nothing to do with football. As David Beckham points out in his biography *My Side*, 'It's way past anything to do with football.' In contrast to that well-meaning father who sat next to me at Highfield and had brought his son to the FA Cup to enjoy the spectacle and spend some loving quality time with his little boy, this glaring thug was hoping to create a spectacle of his own and unleash a tornado of frustration onto the faceless fans of this week's opposition. If, as philosopher John Ralston Saul argues, insanity 'is our loss of our sense of the other', this man was, even momentarily, on the brink of an insane act.

Instead of blaming, castigating and taking it all out on, say, an abusive father, a class system that perpetuates inequality or a boss who has unfairly dismissed you, contempt for the status quo was about to be transmuted onto this week's perceived enemy – the players and members of the opposition, as well as any symbols of authority who stood in the way (that is, the poor referee) – all of whom had *nothing to do with its initial cause.*

You couldn't pay refs enough these days.

In the video store last week, I picked up *Hooligans & Thugs: Soccer's Most Violent Fan Fights, Narrated by Steve Jones 'The Original Punk Rocker'.* Much like those *Greatest Goals of the Decade* collections, this deplorable disc showed a collection of the Greatest Moments of Mindless Fan Violence, tightly edited to fifty-eight gratuitous minutes with a beat-box soundtrack and peppered with Jones, costumed as a knight and a bobby, presenting a pro-British commentary which tried unconvincingly to sound as though he was detached from it all. I then noticed in the Aussie Rules section that Rex Hunt had a DVD entitled *Biffs, Bumps and Brawlers*. Same sort of silly stuff. Different code. Bugger the sporting event – it would seem the antics of the freaks and their sideshows are more entertaining than the actual sport. In promoting this muck as entertainment, I fear we are giving it too much street credibility and sowing some very dangerous antisocial seeds as to what is acceptable behaviour both for players and spectators. The kid behind the counter (who was also a film critic) told me it was 'a totally awesome video for any sports fan' and that 'it also shifted heaps of units to fans of splatter-fest horror pics'. That somehow did not surprise me. I bought *Hooligans & Thugs* and a 'director's cut' of *Dawn of the Dead*.

Hours later, in front of my flat screen, I had to resist the urge to cheer as these idiots smashed each other over the heads with sticks, destroying the few remaining brain cells that existed there. In truth, at key points, I wasn't clear which film I was actually watching. But when footage of the Heysel tragedy of 1985 was shown (where thirty-nine Juventus fans were crushed to death due to crowd insurgence prior to the European Cup final against Liverpool), I lost my sense of humour and found myself praying for a world where this type of behaviour didn't exist. And where DVDs like these need not be made.

Shame on you, Steve. Shame on you, Rex. And shame on me for forking out my hard-earned cash to buy the thing in the first place.

At the end of *Hooligans & Thugs*, 'The Original Punk Rocker' impassively asks, 'You learnt anything?' Then mutters, lifting himself off a toilet seat and pulling up his pants, 'Probably not.'

André Agassi once remarked that '…when you talk about tennis, you are talking about a sport that transcends the lines of life'. He's not correct, you know. It just *seems* like it. Tennis is just a game with a bizarre scoring system and fuzzy, fluoro-coloured balls that you whack with cat gut.

Sport is not about life and death. Let's get that much clear. It just seems that way sometimes and we like to *pretend* that it is so. And when many diverse and interesting people continue to 'throw their hearts' into it – as well as a hell of a lot of money, a myriad of expectations, agendas, politics, dreams, and so on – there will always be outcomes where the spirit emerges triumphant and stories of where the spirit is left totally bankrupt. When cast against the backdrop of life and death matters, we need to remember that it is just a game, originally invented in order to divert our attentions away from all this goo and heaviness. As a character noted with some irony in Tibor Fischer's novel *Under the Frog*, set in the years leading up to the Hungarian uprising of 1956, 'Hungarians don't mind dictatorship, but they really hate losing a football match.' One would perhaps prefer that they hated the dictatorship but didn't mind the outcome of a football match. Then at least they'd be reacting against the real source of their feeling of loss and hopelessness. And maybe get to possibly enjoy the distraction which sport can provide.

In reflecting on the eccentricities of the British during his marvellous, televised version of *Notes from a Small Island*, the irrepressible Bill Bryson reminds us to keep things in important perspective:

> No other nation has given the world more games than Britain: football, rugby, golf, tennis, cricket. Never mind that very often – pretty generally in fact – the rest of the world beats you at these games. There's a reason for this, I think. Unlike other nations, the British almost never fail to forget that it is, after all, just a game.

I like to think that, in most cases, Bryson has got it right and that the evening we experienced in Coventry was nothing but an aberration.

Training Module 3
Clubbing

Leeds is a great club and it's been my home for
years, even though I live in Middlesbrough.

Jonathan Woodgate

Germany are a very difficult team to play. They had
11 internationals out there today.

Steve Lomas

The way I see it, it works like this.

When you associate yourself with a player or team,
as Mamet stated, you invest, indulge and project a
part of yourself in them. You personalise the game. In
post-match banter, fans always talk about their team
in personal terms: *We didn't play well* or *We dominated
the game in the second half.* I always find this amusing as
'we' pretty much didn't do anything but sit on our arse,
yell a lot and eat over-priced hot dogs. As it is better 'to
invest' with a lot of like-minded people, strong bonds
are usually formed with those around you in the stands.
Some of my closest friendships have been made and

cemented through these sporting 'families'. (It is also why I despair at those parents, players and supporters who change from club to club whenever they do not get their way or do not have instant success. They will never know the value of lasting allegiance.) This concept of family and belonging also creates a safety net. I'm no economist, but I imagine this theory works the same with shares.

These folk hence become your 'club', in the real sense of the word and irrespective of whether it is owned in name or funded by a rich investor, some other governing body or an authoritative institution. You *belong* and consequently share in the elation and agony of whatever occurs come match day. While at Liverpool, Bill Shankly tried to break down the hierarchical barriers which existed within his club when he famously proclaimed from his perch as manager,

> I'm just one of the people who stands on the kop. They think the same as I do, and I think the same as they do. It's a kind of marriage of people who like each other.

And you do generally stay married to your 'club' – these people who you like and are like you – unless other seemingly pertinent life and death matters push you to be divorced, ostracised or estranged from it. As David Beckham comments on the strength of this marriage,

> There are plenty of football supporters in England who

would rather see their club win the League than see the National team win the World Cup. I can understand that. You follow your club 365 days of every year; you're thinking and talking about it far more than the England side. Everybody gets involved when England are playing in the major tournaments and big games, but your passion for the team you support is there all the time.

This unification of people can be very strong. I like the way some clubs append the word 'United' to the end of their names. It does suggest a common bond and goal, even if that is to pulverise everybody else. While that may not be totally fair, as Coventry City supporters like me are just happy for their team to maintain its essentially winless existence, I am not alone in loving a loveless side. I recently spotted a delightful *Canberra Times* article by Exeter City's only Australian fan, Graham Cooke, entitled 'Win or lose I love my team'. Exeter gave Manchester United an honest scare in their third round 2005 FA Cup replay. (Obviously third round FA Cup ties are where things really happen.) Although the bigger club learnt an important lesson about underestimating the spirit of a small club from Devon (after a scoreless first tie), despite winning the replay 2–0 (after a big struggle), Cooke insisted,

When I die a post mortem will reveal that 'Exeter City' is written across my heart. Then I want to be cremated and my ashes scattered on St James Park. You see, I don't care that the City are playing at the fifth level of English soccer, or that in 101 years the national trophy haul is one Fourth Division championship. The United replay didn't work out, but on the following day more than 100 people answered an appeal to help clear up the mess left on the terraces. They are the true football supporters, the best sportspeople, ever hopeful of a win, yet a loss – or 10 losses in a row – makes them love their team not a jot the less.

With supporters like these, clubs certainly do not deserve to be relegated, denigrated and/or die, in whatever division, league or competition they may dwell.

Clubs tend to be linked to either a geographic region such as a suburb, a region or city, a state, a nation, a block of nations, or most of the planet (for example, West Woden Under 8s, Southside Under 8s, ACT Under 8s, Australian Under 8s, South Pacific Under 8s, The Rest of the World Under 8s); an institution such as a school, a university or work place (Radford First XI, University of Canberra Youth, Public Service Paper Pushing XI); some influence of patronage or sponsorship (the Prime Minister's XI or Darren's Dial-a-Pizza Deliverers); an age, gender or even sexual preference (Southside Senescence Society, West Woden Waspish Women or The Galloping Gays of Gowrie); skill level (The Hotshots, The ACT Academy of Soccer or – and this is my favourite – The

Mixed Vegetables); or less wisely by a religion, a political standpoint or even a philosophy (Southside Sikhs, Team Green or the Low-noise Side of Silence Special XI). This linkage, while important in defining the club's 'investors' in terms of its people, place and/or perceptions, carries with it some inherent difficulties, especially when groups defined by contrasting cultural, ideological or political (to choose three) systems are pitted against each other.

As a wise person once intimated, the soup gets all thick and bubbly when the ingredients are, for instance, religion and politics. Fixtures such as Sikh vs Hindu, Private Schools vs Government Schools, Secular vs Non-Secular, Separatists vs Loyalists, Blacks vs Whites, Democrats vs Autocrats, Representative Teams vs Club Sides, The US Embassy vs the Iranian Embassy, to name a few, are all match-ups potentially asking for some degree of trouble. And even fixtures between the like-minded, as we all know, can be just as equally and negatively charged, like a Civil War. When I coached one of two ACT Futsal sides in both 2002 and 2003, there was little love lost between the two sides whenever they had to play each other in the finals at the Nationals. The same could be said when Radford College plays Marist College (two Christian Canberra private schools, one co-ed and Anglican, the other boys only and Catholic); they quite happily go for each other's throats every time they play, despite many of Jesus's messages of restraint and peace. And is there any love lost between Carlton and Collingwood? Enough said.

And then you can still up the ante.

When a 'club' or team represents a *country* it advertently and inadvertently defends, promotes and represents a notion of its culture, politics, ideology and even religion in the more extreme cases. Matches between India and Pakistan, England and Scotland, and USA with most of the world, for example, can become heated affairs because of their social, political and historical backdrop. So, whenever a sporting fixture takes place between countries, we need to strongly resist the temptation of assuming that *a measly game* implies any sort of superiority or domination with respect to any of these notions.

For instance, if the USA defeats Iraq in an international ping-pong one-off test, it does not and must not imply that one country is a wiser military superpower or that 'democracy' is a necessarily victorious, sensible and sole style of politics; if Radford (an independent school) defeats a government school in The Bill Turner Soccer Cup, it should never imply that the standards of education, co-curricular activities, uniform policy or even resources are better at the private institution; and if Darren's Dial-a-Pizza Deliverers or the uncanny Side of Silence Special XI pull through (with and without telepathy) in their round matches, it does not necessarily follow that Darren's pizzas are exceptionally scrumptious and nutritious or that not making a single utterance on the pitch is a good thing.

Of course, in the modern era, the conflict can become clouded off the field as well in the whole tiresome 'club versus country' controversy. Clubs which pay exorbitant amounts for their international superstars get very shirty when these superstars need to leave town to play fixtures for their countries, especially if the fixture is perceived to be irrelevant by the club.

On a smaller scale, I have often experienced representative junior players missing trainings and weeks of club games so as not to risk injury and damage their chances to play in representative fixtures. Where present and future careers and employment prospects are on the line, these conflicts are not easily resolved.

While it is impossible to totally stop wider social, political and historical implications and undertones from appearing in and around sport, we should at least be wary and cognisant of their side-effects. One toxic side-product is that sport can sometimes shut the door on those who love it but who have no affiliation or concern with a chosen club's hidden and not-so-hidden agenda.

When Australia's National Soccer League formed in 1977, club names were to have no ethnic identity as a condition of entry. For example, Sydney Croatia had to become Sydney United. The club's board and members were understandably incensed because they were largely responsible for the formation and longevity of the club and did not like being told what to do. What they failed to understand was that, while they owned the club, they did not own the sport. Sadly, if not paradoxically, the only thing which essentially became 'United' were the Croatians at the club against not only the interfering football administrators, but everyone outside of the club who wanted 'in' on this growing sport.

In *Shoot Out*, soccer analyst Ross Solly explains how *The Stewart Report*

> ...found the administration of individual soccer clubs almost exclusively ethnically based, which in the past had been a strength of the sport. But now, Stewart decided, that same ethnically-based infrastructure was a substantial weakness in promoting soccer nationally.

Former Soccer Australia Chairman David Hill acted on this sort of advice and ordered the removal of all European insignia from playing strips and fields. When he attended a Sydney United game during his time on the SA board, he was surprised to hear all the ground announcements being delivered in Croatian and the pre-match entertainment celebrating, commemorating and venerating red and white chequers:

> You honestly felt like groping for a visa or a passport to get in... Nobody ever went there unless you had a Croatian connection. You weren't made feel welcome.

But in trying to make the game more mainstream and accessible to people outside of these strong ethnic communities, he met with aggressive opposition.

As a clumsy kid in the late seventies, I was advised not to bother trialling for Croatia Deakin as they did not field lower-division teams. (As an adult, I think they should be made to as a condition of playing in the ACT Junior League.) I was directed towards 'The Italians'. I was then told at West Woden Juventus I would never make it as a player because I had no Azzurri blood in me. When I said I was Dutch, it was met with a great deal of laughter and a series of amusing adult jokes about clogs and dykes. I asked Dad what I need do to become Italian and, after cooking me a spaghetti, he took me to the first of many visits to Deakin Oval to witness the spiteful games between Croatia Deakin and West Woden Juventus. I can recall feeling that Dad and I were the only people at the game interested in the quality of the football being played. Here were two sides exhibiting a unique and contrasting brand of soccer with flair, skill and ingenuity. They were gifted to a man, and many like

John Janeczko, Ivan Gruicic and Walter Valeri became my childhood heroes. Yet everyone around me seemed more concerned with arguing, both verbally and physically, about whether being Croatian or Italian was the best thing for a person to be. I noted that very few people at Deakin Oval ever watched the game.

The fights that inevitably broke out between supporters were rarely – if ever – about the football, more about racial differences, sexual prowess and political complexities which, as a seven-year-old, I had little hope of comprehending. From the safety of Australia in the seventies, little Georgie did not understand why anyone need be so angry and violent because somebody else originated from another spot on the globe. (The seeds of my discomfort with extreme nationalism were born there and then.) And I remember thinking, at the tender age of seven, that these people must have come from a very unhappy past if winning this little Canberran Division 1 soccer match mattered so much more than anything else in life. Including the actual *enjoyment* of a weekend football game which so often had beautiful if not magical skills on regular display. I watched both the Deakin and West Woden 'keepers intently over these years and took the best bits from both of their techniques back to my training ground. I might never become truly Croatian or Italian, but I assumed I was still able to become a good goalie.

As Les Murray states in *Mr and Mrs Soccer*,

> For me, the benefit of ethnic involvement was in furthering the cause of the game, not the community…
> I disagreed with any notion that Italianness or Hungarianness was more important than the game. I could still be a proud Hungarian without holding the well-being of football to ransom.

If success by the tired definition held by so many numbskulls from the club to country level implies power, domination, supremacy and an assumed *right* to victory at the expense of others, wherever this definition holds sway I grant you that thuggery, hooliganism and patriotism (in the suspect sense of the word) are rarely far behind in a crowd, like the trio of gutless wonders they are. That's why thugs, hooligans and extreme patriots characteristically engage in hurling coins, cans and bricks, spit from balconies, pick fights in gangs, point firecrackers and even shoot guns. Because they're shrouded in the safety of the crowd and are a safe distance from whoever or whatever they've randomly propelled their missiles at. They are intrinsically gutless. That is why we should applaud those police cameras that pick out individuals in throbbing, recalcitrant mobs – because no longer can these great big chickens hide in the anonymity of a large crowd.

These are not the sort of people you truly want 'behind' your club. As Shankly went on to say about an unsupportive chairman, 'I want you in front of me. Not behind me.'

So here is my next statement of intent.

I propose the formation of a club which wants to maintain, celebrate and promote humanity, better living and *kaizen* through sport, over and above any other association, affiliation or whatnot. It will have no dull, wordy and loophole-ridden constitutions, no dreary monthly meetings and minutes, and cost nothing to join. In fact, anyone can offer membership to anyone else, anywhere, at any time. It will be a loose 'kind of marriage of people' (thanks, Shankly!) who will recognise and look out for each other everywhere, particularly on weekends. It will go to games to enjoy the beauty and distraction of sport...and for no other reason. It will leave politics, religion and other social concerns to fight amongst themselves in boardrooms until they spontaneously combust. It will refuse classification or definition and need not be sanctioned by any bunch of suits. No jackals allowed.

Dear reader, you are already a life member.

Training Module 4
Rage Against the Machine

What dehumanizes you inexorably dehumanizes
me.

Desmond Tutu, *No Future Without Forgiveness*, 1999.

Here I am expecting just a little bit too much from
the wounded.

A Perfect Circle, *3 Libras*, 2000.

Referees don't stand a chance.

The poor officials, at all levels, are absolutely guaranteed
to receive a metaphorical if not metaphysical clubbing
each and every game, and I can't see it changing for
thousands of years. In his book *On Football* (in a chapter
accurately entitled 'The Unloved Ones'), Michael
Parkinson recounts a village derby where a player
named Blackie, who apparently had not been sent off
in fifteen years of playing, felled the referee with a right
hook when he received the dreaded red card. He figured
he might as well make the punishment fit the crime.
Disturbingly, the player was not all that perturbed by

the consequent life ban he received and the club even ran a charity game for him:

> The posters advertising the game said 'Proceeds for a deserving tragedy' because they couldn't announce they were collecting for a banned player. The referee, on the other hand, got little sympathy from anyone, and eventually went to live in Wakefield. If you go back to the village now, they'll still point Blackie out to you, and tell you how he fixed the referee.

I must admit to being guilty myself of recounting stories from my youth (and, er, beyond) of my infamous yet questionably entertaining moments of intimacy with referees of many codes. Quite pathetic, really, but good for a cheap laugh and scallywag points.

If Mother Teresa reffed a village Junior League derby in any code she'd get accused of being biased, one-eyed, ineffectual, possibly racist and lacking any moral fibre. As *each and every* spectator and player and team and club and country – especially the vociferous ones – demand to know why the poor official has failed to recognise their own personal needs, complaints and agendas as the singularly most important ones at the venue, the referee has absolutely no hope of appeasing anyone.

Ironically, referees are frequently distracted from doing a good job by all the constant and increasingly dynamic submissions of grievance proffered throughout a match.

Also ironic is the fact that, while soccer has slowly become the sport Australians prefer to play (eclipsing cricket in a Bureau of Statistics and Roy Morgan poll), referee retention is radically decreasing. In July 2004, NSW Soccer Referees state secretary, Ron Beaumont, indicated in the *Sydney Morning Herald* that each year about 1,000 of the 3,500 referees in NSW drop out of the game. While refs get injured, relocate and develop other interests, it does not take a genius to postulate why this trend is occurring.

I think I speak for most of us when I say that if sport becomes lifelike – and we've ascertained that it does in those intense moments on the field – it puts too much pressure on the referee to read it correctly. So when the ref makes a decision, especially when it is contrary to our wishes, we generally take it as a personal affront and a deliberate, conscious impediment to our wishes. That's when all hell starts breakin' loose. We can rant and rave at referees for not being on our side but (without wishing to be too cosmic) there are deeper issues of blame at work here which need *not* be addressed by the referee. We should be ranting and raving over fate and destiny at priests, soothsayers or whoever or whatever created us in the first place. It's their job to find the answers, more so than referees. And metaphysical questions are better asked of your guru, yoga instructor, gardener, hairdresser, taxi driver or directly of God herself rather than a ref. The referee is no Divine Mediator of the Universe who can provide us with any significant, lasting and profound enlightenment to take back with us into our regular lives. The ref can only give us their fallible, humble and human opinion on an offside decision.

It seems a natural, human conceit not to react pleasantly to those in authority telling us, controlling us, advising us or even deciding for us important things to do with sport, let alone in life. As a schoolteacher, I have had some experience with this. *But we need mediators in life and we need human ones.* There is a lot of argument about video refs and action replays but, the way I see it, we'll never afford, both financially and spiritually, to have that sort of technology at the West Woden Under 8 Division 3 side's fixtures – and I'm not sure they should have them for professional sporting events either. Despite the big money and egos involved.

Why should we have technology at games? So that we don't 'take things out' on the ref? So we can 'take things out' on a machine instead? For pinpoint accuracy in decision-making? To settle arguments? To be *certain*? Yet when things are a dead heat, a line ball or seem totally unseparable, don't we then return to the human fourth umpire for a decision anyway? It would be a sad day when any junior sports code resorts to taping games to settle any potential disputes. For better or worse, we are in the ref's hands, whether we like it or not. This call to be mediated by a machine rather than a human is doing nothing short of lauding the *dehumanising* of sport which is occurring every week and as we speak.

Much as I love The Green Machine, admire The Scud and want to be an Iron Man chick-magnet, there's something a little too metallic implied in these names. To me, there's something just a bit too cold in being likened to a collection of steel nuts, bolts and screws. These terms mechanise, depersonalise, serialise and figuratively castrate people and teams of any personality and character. (It never surprised me that one of the most nasty, insatiable and omnipotent villains in *Star Trek: The Next Generation* was The Borg – an organic and ruthless computer system intent on assimilating everything into its wicked, bland, faceless collective.) So I wonder if part of the reason sport stars visit sick fans in hospitals and wide-eyed kiddies at primary schools is that they are melting through all the steel, making a concerted attempt to realign themselves with their community and thus their own humanity. I hope so.

In short, this demand for 'getting things totally right'

is, at its best, infantile, selfish and a hindrance to sport's reaching towards and touching its intrinsic humanity. And perhaps the wider lesson here is that in our inaccurate, argumentative and uncertain lives we are also so often left in the metaphorical 'hands of others' – a teacher, a boss, some authoritative system. Sometimes these 'hands' (and bodies) work with us, at other times they can slap us and beat us down. Yet sport can teach us how to cope when things go wrong, awry and poorly – especially when things go wrong, awry and poorly in *a measly game*. So why try to smooth out all the rough edges?

How we choose to react to important or inconsequential, correct or incorrect decisions, moments and influences in our life is what *living* is actually about. Sport allows us a training ground to practise life matters, often with the like-minded, so that when we are confronted by these weighty matters outside of the sportsgrounds, we are better equipped to handle them. And maybe work together to overcome them.

And perhaps, also, to accept them. Then get on with it.

Training Module 5
Dad vs Dad

Hatred passed on, passed on and passed on
A world of violent rage
But it's one that I can recognise
Having never seen the colour of my father's eyes.
  Rage Against the Machine, *Settle for Nothing*, 1992.

You can pick up the paper most days and read about some bizarre manifestation of sporting anger. On 1 July 2003, I did just that and found the following in *The Canberra Times*:

An Iranian footballer reportedly killed a player from the opposing side who had just scored a goal by punching him in the head. The *Yas-e No* daily newspaper yesterday said an amateur soccer match in Ahwaz in the south-west last Friday turned ugly… The victim was carried from the pitch and when his death was announced over loudspeakers the attacker was detained by the opposing team and handed over to the police.

Have you noticed that if you search frantically for a

story on good sportsmanship you'll come up with bugger all?

And few were possibly more tragic than in 2002 when a 270-pound truckie, Thomas Junta, was convicted of involuntary manslaughter by a jury in Cambridge, Massachusetts, and was sentenced to six to ten years in prison. It all happened at the Burbank Ice Arena in Reading, Massachusetts, during a junior ice hockey match. Unhappy with some rough checking that had been apparently inflicted on his ten-year-old son, Quinlan, Junta approached the coach, Michael Costin, who had been officiating. Costin's response to Junta's complaint was 'That's what hockey's all about.' Junta returned moments later and, in front of both his son Quinlan and Costin's three sons, Brendan, twelve, Michael, eleven, and Sean, ten, physically assaulted the coach. As recorded in *Sports Illustrated* in January the following year:

> He (Junta) then began beating Costin's face with his fists and banging his head on the hard rubber mats that covered the floor. Costin's three boys stood around Junta screaming, 'Please stop! Please! He can't see. He can't hear.' Junta did not stop, prosecutors say, until a bystander pulled him off. By the time police arrived, Costin lay unconscious, without a pulse, his head in a pool of blood, his face misshapen by the blows.

Is there something sinisterly primal lingering in the

back alleys of Sport Street? What is it in sport which can unleash all this blind, mindless and pent-up aggression? When reflecting on the Junta case, Douglas Abrams, a law professor at the University of Missouri, whose interest lies in following the profound stupidity of idiot spectators right across the USA, stated,

> These parents push and shove. If they were your next-door neighbour, you'd like them. But when somebody yells 'Play ball!' something happens.

Something happens all right. What is that unsweet 'something'?

There is evidently 'something' in Mamet's theory that we each 'rationalise, objectify and personalise the process of the game'. Add to that – and I want to state categorically that I have been victim to this myself – that as soon as a starting whistle is blown, we are incredibly more susceptible to having our own sense of *personal justice* bloated totally out of proportion to the magnitude of what is actually going on in front of us. How else could a junior sporting match provoke such irrelevant and irreverent frustration in the mild and the not-so-mild mannered? How else could a kiddies' ice hockey match end up in pointless bloodshed? Just think about the last time you encountered any injustice on a sportsfield. An aggrieved spectator or coach can quickly and passionately articulate quite coherent and damning statements of perceived 'fact' outlining why their team has been 'unjustly done by', usually to any referee or hapless bystander, while rarely recognising that the opposition side could do exactly the same thing (and generally do) equally convincingly from the other side of the field.

This is because sport, in its nifty, cheeky and multifaceted little fence-sitting way, requires conflict, challenge and obstacles. Looking at it logically, the very nature of sport requires that two 'sides' are actually *around* for it to take place. A marathon runner has to work *against* something, even if it is his stopwatch, some niggling pain or his body screaming for him to take a fast right into the local pub for a Guinness from Cheryl, the cute barmaid. Even playing Solitaire you have this sense of playing against something, even if it is fate. Hence, at every weekend sporting event, conflicting desires, emotions and bodies are constantly hurled against each other for an hour or two (or a day or five in the case of cricket). The pessimists and cynics around us will concur that this is when we need only wait for something potentially unbecoming and/or stupidly dangerous to happen.

It's a lesser known fact that Thomas Junta and Michael

Costin both had prison records. As *Sports Illustrated* revealed,

> Neither Junta nor Costin was new to the criminal justice system. Costin had been in prison seven times between 1983 and 1995 for crimes that stretched from breaking and entering to assaulting a cop, and Reading police believe he had ties to a gang of Hell's Angels in nearby Lynn, Mass. Junta had been charged with but found not guilty of wilful destruction of property, had been sentenced to a year in jail for using a vehicle without the owner's permission and, in 1992, had been arrested for assault and battery. (There was no disposition in that case.)

So, one could assume that both these men brought to their respective roles of 'spectator' and 'official' some baggage and possible disgruntlement for the law and/or society. Again, what a recipe for disaster. If both were convinced, again as Mamet suggested, that they were the (dubious) heroes of their own lives while bringing – as I've suggested – their warped personal sense of justice, Junta quite probably would have *felt* that he was *totally justified* in bashing Costin to death.

At least until the blood dried.

When I was somewhat hypocritically telling off a parent (a dad again!) on the sidelines two weekends ago for berating a young referee, this gentleman had some pretty nasty things to say to me about my appearance and perceived sexuality, punctuating it with a ferocious glare which suggested it was very likely he was going to pummel me into the dirt at any given moment. (He stalked me after the match until he realised I was actually the coach of sixteen very extra-large Under 17 players training behind the goal a few metres away.) I imagine, if we were in some dark alley, he might well have happily bashed me senseless. He would have rationally figured that he was justified in doing so because I was 'a dickhead' with the gall to question his sense of justice, perspective and self. In essence, I had the cheek to disagree with him about how he was conducting himself as a person of responsibility both as a spectator and a father.

Oh, and like Junta, he probably would have had his kids in tow while he beat me up.

Tennis fathers are a notorious lot. Jelena Dokic and Jennifer Capriati both have had well-documented fathers-from-hell. But by far my personal favourite is Jim Pierce, father of French sensation, Mary. As Doug Conway wrote in an worrying article entitled 'A Parent from Hell?',

Mary Pierce's dad would slap her after she lost a match, and sometimes even if she had a bad practice. He punched two spectators at the French Open and once yelled out from the stands, 'Mary, kill the bitch!' His behaviour prompted what is known as the Jim Pierce Rule prohibiting abuse from coaches and relatives.

It is sadly clear that the only person involved in the sorry shenanigans outlined above who needed a good slapping or punching was Jim Pierce himself. Like Costin, Junta and the sideline pugilist I told off recently, the personal connection not only to the game but to *the family member playing it*, seemed to exacerbate and amplify the largely unresolved ugliness and aggro that already existed inside these unfortunate people.

I picked up a little book entitled *Football Fever* from a bargain bin. It was a delightful little book filled with, well, feverish poems by children about football. Perhaps the only sad aspect of the endearing collection was its young poets' sharp recognition of the 'madness' which can grip its followers. In particular, where this madness gripped family members, the sharp perception flowing out of the mouths of babes became particularly pointed. If, as Anne Bonner suggests in her little poem 'Football', soccer is 'fulfilment of the plain man's dream', it can conversely be seen as the embodiment of any ordinary man's nightmares, depending on whatever occurs on the pitch.

Writes John Whitworth about his grandfather,

Six days a week and he's OK,
A well-behaved old thing.
But on the football Saturday
It's so embarrassing,
A quiet, silver-haired old man
Behaving like a football fan.

He stamps and yells and (oh the shame)
He's even got a rattle.
I tell him how it's just a game.
He acts like it's a battle.
ARSENAL! ARSENAL FOR THE CUP!
Do Grandads ever quite grow up?

Or Daphne Kitching's graver account of her father:

Taking sides,
swearing, jostling
Threatening more…
Anger grown out of singing,
Turning to hatred of different colours.
'Be polite and kind.'
'Put yourself in their shoes.'
'A smile costs nothing.'
'Respect others.'

Lessons from another world
Before the madness of the match
Transformed my dad.

As dear Daphne insinuates, it is almost as if sport

requires one to leave manners, etiquette, ideals, a sense of perspective and even humanity at the turnstile on arrival. These are sadly lessons from another world. It is quite awful when you consider Daphne is also writing about her own father, whose double standards have hardly met the criteria he himself set and should abide by as a father and/or responsible adult. Isn't it terrible when it is our children who remind us about our hypocrisy?

When browsing (again) through *The Canberra Times* during my holidays, I found a plethora of ridiculous articles such as the following, which suggested that the Junta scenario could just as easily have enacted itself on our sunburnt shores:

> A Melbourne man needed emergency surgery to remove 10cm of umbrella spoke from his back after a fight at a children's soccer game, police said yesterday. The piece of umbrella spoke was embedded in the man's lower back in an altercation with another parent while the two men watched an Under 11 soccer game at Caloola Reserve, Oakleigh, in Melbourne's south-east, on Sunday. The men's sons were on opposing teams in the match.

Might I suggest that it is often fathers, burdened with having to keep their testosterone in check all week at the office where there are other discerning grown-ups, who are investing far too much vicarious and vicious passion into their children's games on Saturdays. These two silly Victorian men were evidently bringing with them more than just parasols and a deep-rooted desire to 'fulfil their dreams' when they stepped out of their suburban homes an hour before their kids' game. To them, it would seem, how their offspring played in a measly game was obviously a value judgement on their parenting skills and, more significantly, a direct psychological extension of their own vicarious need for success, affirmation and validation.

In his unforgettable biography *Full Time*, Irish international Tony Cascarino describes how, when he was nine, his father came to watch one of his soccer games:

> We were hammered 7–2 and he did nothing but shout at me all through the game. It was miserable. I could see all the other parents looking at him and towards the end I completely lost it and told him to give me a break. He brought me home and gave me a beating. He swore he would never come and watch me again and as ever was as good as his word. The experience left me physically and emotionally scarred. The bruises quickly healed but the emotional wounds lingered. I performed poorly in school and generally lacked confidence. I wet the bed until I was fourteen years old.

Cascarino goes on to describe the lovelessness he sensed at his grandparents' home and how his father, unskilled, unqualified and illiterate spent the majority of his working life 'ducking and diving to survive'.

Then, instead of using a game as an opportunity to duck and dive from grim reality and inch a little closer to his impressionable young son, it evidently just became another sad opportunity for him to vent his spleen, unleash some pent-up anger, estrange himself from his boy and ultimately confirm his own hopelessness. One can only postulate what might have happened if the scores were reversed. Possibly it would just have kept the demons at bay for another week.

But just in case mothers think I am letting women off the hook, I hardly think the Ugly Parent Syndrome need be confined to mere males. A parent of one of my charges sent me the following article from the Internet:

> Soccer mum Christine X admits she could be seen as a 'difficult parent'. But this time Mrs X's sideline antics have gone too far, costing her 16-year-old daughter the chance to represent Australia. Despite being voted Best and Fairest and Miss Congenial by her soccer team-mates, Anne-Elise X has been dumped from the Queensland representative team after she was forced to come to her mother's rescue in a sideline altercation at a premier match in Toowoomba last month.
>
> Women's Soccer Queensland deemed Anne-Elise an 'unacceptable risk' after she shoved a woman who she claims was about to push her outspoken mother down a flight of stairs. While Anne-Elise admits to pushing the woman, Mrs X claims she was the one to blame and her daughter has been unfairly punished.

'I think they are trying to get back at me but they can't get back at me so they've punished her,' Mrs X said. 'I guess I could be conceived as a difficult parent... I am just fiercely supportive.'

My answer to how we can remove all this parasol-waving and throwing-downstairs will be handled ingenuously in the next Training Module and grappled with more seriously in the remainder of this book.

But in the interim, might I suggest we get someone at the AIS to develop a Genuine Disturbance Indicator (GDI), a small machine something like a lie detector which every player or supporter at a sports event needs to be scanned with prior to their arrival at the venue. We also need to strip search suspects for sharp, pointy and waterproofing implements. If the needle discovers any sense of psychological disturbance in the force – for instance, the potential to send someone hurling down a series of stairwells – we hand them an ambient CD of waves breaking and birds singing, ask them to leave their umbrellas with us, and suggest they go home and put on the kettle.

Training Module 6
Leaving Jackals at the Gate

Ancient Egyptians believed they were gods of the underworld, and that their evening yips and yowls were the haunting songs of the dead. Modern cultures dismissed them as cold-hearted and calculated killers, the vicious thugs of the animal world. But as Nature's 'Jackals of the African crater' shows, the dog-like jackal lives a far more complicated – and challenging – life than many once believed.

Nature On-Line, 'Jackals of the African Crater', 2003

A GDI would have gone haywire at the 2005 National futsal titles held in Canberra. I had been coaching an Under 11 ACT squad. After a reasonably close loss to another unnamed state, the fans of the opposition side began their post-match tribal stuff. The players were delightful and began a little circular jig with each other. Good for them. But they were not the problem.

At the full-time whistle, a visiting and victorious father let out a full-pitched howl with his mouth as agape as the entrance to Luna Park. The nerves on his forehead were writhing like snakes. The intensity was so massive that cracks started appearing in the ceiling. His scream was angry, joyless and strangely full of vindication – as if my Under 11s were responsible for some war atrocity which resulted in the torture and death of his loved ones – and these dastardly perpetrators were finally receiving some ultimate retribution here in a little Canberran indoor sports centre. Then the remaining supporters all gathered together and clasped each other desperately, close to tears, as if a judge had pronounced the death sentence on a serial killer. This was not a celebration of the outcome of a closely fought junior futsal game. No. There was a deeper, desperate sense of having defeated something evil inside and outside of themselves. Momentarily, through this little win, the jackals had dominated over something in their possibly joyless lives which had nothing to do with futsal or little boys. Unfortunately, it made my losing eleven-year-olds feel like crap.

I looked at my 'serial killers' who were down but not destroyed (as we were well-practised at needing to bounce back). I felt compelled to ask Mr Edvard Munch if we had done something unforgivable to him in a past life. To maybe request that he pipe down with his Braveheartisms as he was making my diminutive troopers feel like they were the bad guys. But instead I went and shook his hand, dryly commented that he was obviously very 'happy' that he had won and decided to spend my remaining post-match energy to help my Under 11s understand the relative insignificance of the loss in a pool match. And explain to them that when they win a game they are actually allowed to *enjoy* it rather than employ it as some sort of spiritual laxative.

In contrast, I recount with greater pleasure how the *Sydney Morning Herald* writer Peter FitzSimons heard (from a reader) about a priceless curtain-raiser to an inner city grand final between two Under 9 sides. An Abbotsford side was down by two goals in a match where the parents of both sides were screaming their lungs out at the poor kids and adding fuel to an already tense situation. Somewhat bravely, the Abbotsford coach collected his side together and led them in a round of 'If you're happy and you know it clap your hands'. As FitzSimons reported,

> The Abbotsford team went out in the second half and proceeded to score three unanswered goals, thus winning the game, sending the team and the coach back into another chorus of 'If you're happy and you know it, clap your hands'. It was an amazing sight, and I only wish I had a coach like that.

Last year, my little Radford Under 12s participated at the futsal Schools Nationals in Brisbane and would do a little Jamaican dance and make up nonsense rhymes suggesting they could bake really good cakes as well as play excellent futsal and that we were going to steal the opposition's girlfriends as well as the game. I noted with pride that a couple of these little legends went on to be selected in a Futsal ACT representative side for the recent Nationals and had introduced a bizarre Hawaiian hand-waving dance entitled 'Salute to the Sun' to their stunned teammates, requesting them to perform their funky, solar salutation prior to important games. While many may think that this is idiotic behaviour, I think it's extremely commendable. If anything, it reminds all and sundry at the junior sporting event that we are dealing with kids and that it doesn't hurt to have a bit of fun, enjoyment and entertainment at something which is increasingly becoming far too serious for its own good. So if you're happy – and you know it – clap or wave those happy hands and do a little solar-powered dance...

Go on.

So do I have a solution for all this nonsense?

Yup. We need to, in essence, adopt the Jim Pierce rule across all codes and make sure that all participants at a sporting event abide by its rulings. I would also like to propose four light-hearted strategies for keeping the jackals at the gate.

1) *Accept, celebrate and welcome the diversity of needs, hopes and expectations which arrive through the gates each and every week.* Yes, that means go over and welcome oppositions and present them with a hot drink or the metaphoric equivalent. My mother is very good at this. Before an aggrieved person from the home or away side is halfway through a potential diatribe, she's put a thermos cup of steaming Milo into their hands with a 'There, there – drink that up and you'll feel a lot better.' It's harder to get nasty to people once they, or their mother, have been friendly to you in the first instance. (One of my Under 17 players, Billsy, suggested making friends with all the shady people who looked like terrorists before we actually took off on our long-haul flight to England in January 2003. His theory was that they'd be less likely to kill you should a hijacking ever eventuate because you were initially nice to them.)

2) *Promote* kaizen *at all opportunities.* Hand out pamphlets promoting *kaizen* at the turnstiles of entrance gates. Have a *kaizen* merchandise table equipped with souvenir pens, T-shirts, stuffed toys, blow-up dolls and lolly dispensers encouraging the concept of 'continual development'.

3) *Confront any jackals in a non-confronting Gandhi-like manner.* Send someone sweet like a grandmother or a cute four-year-old girl or the Dalai Lama to approach aggressive sideline-pyschos and hand them a card which says,

> Excuse me. Sorry to bother you. But weekend sport is not bringing out the best in you. As controlling your lust for winning is something you are obviously wrestling with (and it would appear that you are losing this fight), we all feel you'd be far better off staying at home with a cup of jasmine tea.

You could also print on the back Anne Bonner's poem from the knockout anthology *Football Fever* (and if a player or spectator is being particularly feral, we can give them a comprehension exercise on the poem...):

Football
is to share.
a game for everyone
everywhere.
Football
should be clean.
Fulfilment
of the plain
man's dream.
Football
should be true.
To loyal fans
like me.
Like you.

Lastly, why not go further and...

4) *Ask every coach, player and spectator to go through some sort of psycho-spiritual evaluation before being allowed to attend sporting functions.* Here is one below. Feel free to copy it and distribute it to all and sundry at your weekend sporting event...

George Huitker's A–Z Questionnaire For Determining If You Should Stay At Home With A Jasmine Tea On Match Days

Just complete the following questionnaire before you leave for a sporting event:

a) If your sporting team loses, do you take it personally?

b) If your sporting team loses, do you feel inferior in any way?

c) If your sporting team loses, do you feel responsible?

d) If your sporting team loses, do you feel the need to hit someone or something or take out some act of dirty little revenge with items such as an umbrella?

e) If your sporting team loses, do you look up at the sky, spin around in a circle with clenched fists and have metaphysical debates with divine powers about why you never get things your way?

f) If your sporting team loses, do you feel it's due to anything but your team's performance?

g) When you yell at referees or players or coaches is

your anger deep-rooted or linked to an unpleasant episode of your childhood?

h) When you yell at referees or players or coaches do you swear or speak in a language, foreign or otherwise, which implies a lot of violence?

i) When you yell at referees or players or coaches are you certain they are primarily responsible for the poor result?

j) Are the officials and the opposition the enemy?

k) Do you feel dirty inside when shaking hands with members of the opposition?

l) Do you feel dirty inside when singing 'Three Cheers' at the end of a fixture?

m) Is winning everything and losing absolutely nothing?

n) Is winning the only road to success?

If the answer is 'no' to all of these, then go to sport with my blessing. Then try these:

o) When you yell at referees does the thought occur to do a course and officiate yourself?

p) When you yell at players does the thought occur to you that you couldn't do much better yourself?

q) When you yell at coaches does the thought occur to you that they might love the team as much as you do?

r) When you look up at the sky, spin around in a circle with clenched fists and yell at any divine power about why you never get things your way, has it ever dawned on you that God or whoever may not be all that interested in something as inconsequential as a sporting result?

s) When you brag about sporting success do you feel a little childish?

t) When you are on top of the ladder, do you wonder or remember what it is like to be down at the bottom?

u) When a sports star behaves like a child on television, do you explain to your kids why s/he is a dickhead?

v) When your kids behave like these silly sport stars on television, do you explain to them they are in danger of becoming a dickhead?

w) Is there too much emphasis on winning?

x) Is there too much money in winning?

y) Do you remember what it's like to be a kid?

z) Do you love what you do in sport?

If the answer is 'yes' to all of these, then go to sport with my blessing.

Training Module 7
Taking Penalties

I've handled a lot more emotional things than this in my life... I'm a strong person. Every time somebody hits criticism at me I'll come back fighting.

David Beckham, after his penalty miss in the European Cup Quarter Finals against Portugal, 2004.

Is there any more senseless a way to decide the outcome of a soccer game than penalties?

Most advocates of penalty-taking usually have not been in the situation themselves. At least not recently. They tend to be old men who believe duelling with pistols and firing-up family feuds across generations is a rational way to sort out disputes. I recommend they get out of the boardroom sometime and experience real living and losing. The only possible advantage I can see in penalties is that it makes overpaid professionals earn their money when, after all that extra-time running around, they can inadvertently make a career-staining *pthwerrrt* in front of half the world on satellite TV.

And it seems to be a given fact that even sport-haters love to turn on the television when they can sniff even the faintest whiff of a penalty shoot-out. (I sure as hell do when international hockey is televised.) It's the equivalent of turning on the box to watch the final over in one-day cricket when a small amount of runs are needed for victory with one wicket in hand. I suspect the appeal rests in the fact that fickle TV audience members, like me, are attracted to the intensely dramatic, especially when this sense of dramatic tension has either been enhanced or stifled by a lengthy, drawn-out stalemate. As Johnny Warren states in *Mr and Mrs Soccer*,

Originally it was something television people used to their advantage and it is still a solution they love because they get a result and it is high drama. But it isn't football to me.

It sure isn't.

I can remember the names of most international players who have missed penalties in important matches *purely because they missed their attempt*, and I am far from an avid watcher of the televised game. Possibly, I just empathise deeply with individuals whose one *pthwerrrt* seems to linger like a paint-stripping fart in the player's tunnel. And invariably when it punctuates an otherwise faultless game, season or career. I would assume that any time that particular player next steps up to take a penalty, that person will have to do some pretty hefty psychological fence-building to keep the nagging, neighbouring, nadir of doubt from creeping over the pickets and into the already somewhat harangued psyche. Just ask none other than one of the masters, Roberto Baggio, who wrote in the unambiguously titled 'My Penalty Miss Cost Italy the World Cup?' as late as 2002,

> Only those who have the courage to take a penalty miss them. I failed that time. Period. And it affected me for years. It was the worst moment of my career. I still dream about it. If I could erase a moment from my career, it would be that one.

Geez, Roberto, time to let it go, man. If you miss a penalty these days, just get an on-line casino to sell the offending ball on the internet for over fifty grand.

And ask for a cut.

As a goalkeeper, I created rather than received heartache.

Even as an Under 8, I figured that out-psyching the opposition penalty taker by a) wearing wigs and aprons, b) insinuating that their mother's ability to score was streaks ahead of the actual penalty taker's and c) essentially standing still and listless and nonchalantly hoping for the penalty-taker to crack, would tend to produce positive results for my side. I certainly earned my transfer money for West Woden and some scant respect from my peers.

But more often than not, out-psyching just makes you look like a complete dickhead.

I recall Hans Van Breukelen carrying on like a pork chop before saving a penalty in the Euro 1988 final against Russia. He had a fat and nasty finger-wiggle at the poor little Russian penalty-taker (for 'diving', I assume – Dutch is tough to lip read) and then took hours to step back on his goalie's line because it seemed that Hans thought he was in fact Clint Eastwood in a showdown with the big, bad, ugly Ruskie at high noon. Unfortunately, lanky Hansje just looked like a supreme dag whose lucky moment was about to come. And then, after saving the penalty, he maintained this forced, stony, somewhat constipated face reminiscent of Roger Ramjet when, in truth, all he really did was *guess correctly*. Once again, the poor old Russian loses and returns to his day job flipping patties at McDonald's, Moscow.

Sure you can analyse video tapes of penalty-takers'

preferred sides and modes of penalty-taking, but at the end of the day we are left deciding soccer games with what is essentially a soul-destroying guessing game involving only two players. Rather than the whole team (and coaching staff) being ultimately responsible for its skill, fitness and cohesion – as well as the final outcome of a match – a hapless individual has to step up, take a lottery ticket and hope like hell that s/he hits the ball sweetly or that the goalie dives the wrong way. (Or in my case doesn't dive at all.)

I remember experiencing the abysmal sinking feeling that penalties can produce during the 2001 regional semifinal of the Bill Turner Cup here in Canberra with my Radford side. Adolescent boys take their sport a tad seriously – I think that's pretty well established here. So, when the weight of their team's and the school's (and sometimes the state's) progress hinges on a penalty, you can imagine the toll a miss must take on some unfortunate teen's mental health. In 2001 'we' hit the post twice – with the ball deflecting out instead of in. The opposition balanced the order of the universe by doing the exact opposite.

So then, it essentially all came down to this poor kid who had to take the final kick to keep our hopes alive. Those who had already missed were noticeably absent from the equation at this stage – having dissolved into the anonymity of the team huddle – while the final penalty-taker became the unlucky sod who must ultimately assume the responsibility of creating an outcome: be it as hero or villain. In the case of my 2001 team, I had the feeling Chris was going to miss it as he sauntered towards the box. He did not look at all confident as he stepped up. Then, overawed by the occasion, he produced a flimsy *pthwerrrt* straight at the 'keeper who – like me, decades earlier – barely had to move to make the save. Bugger.

If that sinking feeling of missing isn't enough to make you wanna hurl, you next get the opposition players, coaching staff and supporters erupt in a frenzied outpouring of joy (and relief) metres away from you. This is while you are striving to put on a brave face in front of your teammates who are being unnaturally sympathetic, telling you things like *Heads-up, mate!* or *It's not your fault!* or *We win as a team and lose as a team!* – when all the misser wants to do is find a corner to crawl in, hug themselves, gnaw their arms and uncontrollably weep. In most contexts, you would have to admit that this sort of empathetic advice from the team is genuinely nice, but the person who has just missed the penalty doesn't really assimilate anything at this point but an amplified sense of responsibility for the team's loss at what should or could have been a magic moment.

I spoke to Chris while writing this book and despite the fact he is a centred, life-loving and affable young man about to enter adulthood, the pain from three years ago was still very apparent – even though he had ostensibly gotten over it.

> The team were really nice. But it's a horrible thing for someone to have to go through, particularly a kid. It has some merit – it is a test of your psyche in an pressure situation – but it should be left for when you're more experienced to handle it at an older age.

> If anyone in power in the soccer world reads your book, H, make sure they get rid of penalties in junior soccer. Younger players are generally not ready for this sort of…well…heartache.

Chris indicated that there were even degrees of heartache within the order of penalty-takers. When you miss a penalty, he implied it was harder to come to terms with things the later you take the kick in the process.

> You build up to these big games as a team. But then, suddenly, focus is solely on the person who takes the final kick. Others who went before me and hit the post and missed – it wasn't as bad for them. Their misses weren't the be-all and end-all. Hell. At least my shot was on target! It's just unfortunate that the goalie saved it…

Chris believed that the direct repercussions of his miss

were a decrease in his competitive streak, willpower and motivation to succeed in all sports, not just soccer. Afraid of further failure, he took a refuge of sorts in taking things – if not life – less seriously.

Over the ensuing years, I had seen Chris at times being downright silly on the sportsfield. Perhaps fortuitously, this silliness was directly responsible for us occasionally playing together last year in Radford's Men's Division 7 side (comprising like-minded and silly older-age students, collegians, a teacher who never knew when to stop and my friend Jann who was managing the team and who always pops up when significant soccer events occur along the Soccer Time and Space Continuum). I was happy to see Chris playing, once again, with flair and an unencumbered sense of fun, albeit in the lowest grade imaginable. I gratuitously asked him once if a penalty shoot-out ever eventuated in the finals would he line himself up to take a kick. He gave me a knowing look and said,

It's left me, H. It's forgotten. I just wish it could have worked out better back then for all of us...

I hoped that was the truth. I figured that Father Time somehow provides you with some consolation if you are a patient person. That Radford Men's 7 team, with Chris playing a major part up front, went on to win the 2004 premiership by beating the ANU 2–1. Yet with the scores locked at 1–1 perilously close to the final whistle, I am sure I have some idea as to what might have been going through Chris's mind before the winning goal was eventually scored.

I read, around this time, Charlesworth (my new guru) asserting in *The Coach* that with penalty-taking,

> You must have players who want to do it, who are competent at the task and confident. Sometimes your final choice will hinge on who played well in the game if other things appear equal.

Yet Chris was one of the best players on the paddock that day. Any given two-minute snippet of his play during that semifinal should have immortalised him in the eternal action replay of the memory. But his reward for being left on the paddock for his excellent endeavour was a shitty experience which ruthlessly washed away any of the happier aspects of that day.

Tougher commentators, old farts and gunslingers would say that these things are just a part of life and you have to learn to grow from negative experiences. That may be so. But, at the very least, when it comes to kids, there are some realities of life we can spare them from. Especially *unnecessary* ones…

The Bill Turner competition (an east coast Under 15 interschools competition for boys and girls) almost gets it right.

At full-time, as an extra-time of twenty minutes commences, you start reducing each team's player numbers by one player every five minutes (my feeling is it should be two), restarting with a drop-ball on each occasion. Providing a golden goal is not scored, this then occurs a further two times in extra time, leaving eight players on the pitch at the end of play. (By the way, I have also had the privilege of losing a BT game in this manner, but I can assure all and sundry I felt nowhere near as hideous as I did in 2001. There are normally enough players left on the pitch to assume and share the responsibility for whatever occurs. And my experience has been that player-reduction encourages attacking play.) Johnny Warren, again, agreed with me:

> I have seen many games where the referee sends players from both teams off the field and the game always improves. Player reduction should certainly happen during extra time in tournament matches. I am opposed to the penalty shoot-out…

So why not go the whole hog? Keep reducing the number of players until a result ensues. At least then the responsibility would not be left to a single individual – unless the game is reduced to one-on-one – which is extremely unlikely. More worthy aspects of sport such as fitness, skills and tenacity then become the determining factors of the match.

Baggio and Beckham, to name a couple, have proven on countless occasions that they had the mental mettle to stand tall in intense situations where men are men and sheep are nervous. But even these gifted footballers have found their Achilles heel in the dreaded penalty kick. (Both, in fact, would have been better off facing the wrong direction and kicking it backwards with their heel.) Sure, it may be *the* high-octane, supersonic, ultimate challenge in sport, but for people still developing not only as players but as human beings, the penalty miss is an atrocious and pointless obstacle to leap over and should be eradicated.

I turned to guru Charlesworth for some sense and inspiration in how to negotiate this silly sporting obstacle with any grace. In *The Coach*, he continued to say,

> In some ways this first penalty shoot-out would be a watershed experience for the group. Successfully negotiating it would help redefine the group's belief in itself. Its ability to handle the pressure and intensity of a shoot-out would be instructive.

That is, *if* you successfully negotiate. *If* you *win*. And as far as *kaizen* (development and growth through sport) is concerned, all of the hobbits, adolescents and adults

I have interviewed about missing a penalty – as well as reading the emotions of professional players like Roberto Baggio and David Beckham – are emphatic that the pain *doesn't ever totally leave you*. And to me, that brings it very close to the concept of abuse. Like abusive sideline parents and coaches, it can be a stain on sport which is very hard to totally remove from your system – even after a long period of time. You never really forget not being able to meet the expectations of over-zealous parents and ruthless drill sergeant coaches or the pain of a dream crumbling to pieces after a penalty *pthwerrrt*!

In 2003, my Bill Turner side, without Chris, progressed to the regional semifinals by winning a penalty shoot-out. This time the agony was for someone else. I can remember thinking smugly that these things do balance out in the long run. I desperately wanted to throw my arm around the opposition penalty-misser who laboriously *pthwerrrt*ed the final kick wide of goal and out towards Queanbeyan. I wanted to share his pain and tell him that in three or more years' time it all balances out in the end.

But as his dad directed him, inconsolable with grief, to the car park and a night of bad dreams, I vowed, if it was the last thing I do in junior sport, I would lobby to erase this diabolical practice from soccer.

Training Module 8
Bench Warming

Now you dare to look me in the eye
Those crocodile tears are what you cry
It's a genuine problem you won't try
To work it all out, just pass it by, pass it by

The Who, *Substitute*, 1966

In 1997 I agreed to look after a friend's undefeated softball team when he got posted interstate. Absolutely nobody wanted to take the reins, as the pressure of assuming control of an invincible side (to date) seemed a little too daunting for most. And who could blame them? To any normal person, this was basically asking to be placed in the front line of fire. A veritable hiding to nothing.

Intoxicated by unnecessarily stressful opportunities (I am after all a teacher, junior coach and amateur thespian), I volunteered to look after the team and managed to steer a well-oiled machine into the grand final. Having played rep baseball in my youth, I surprised the boys by having a vague concept as to what was going on. I dutifully gave the entire squad match time, a policy I decided to take into the grand final. I remember a parent questioning me when I put on Pete – who had spent the entire season dropping flies in the outfield and swinging his bat some hours after the ball had actually been pitched – *Are you sure you want to put him on?* (His peers, who were tremendously patient and happy-go-lucky gents, spent a lot of time at practice encouraging Pete to keep his eye on the ball both as a fielder and a batter. They also pushed him – and each other – to dutifully work on improving their sprints between bases and often got me to stand with a stopwatch at first base and time, then record, their runs from the batter's box. I didn't see the point, but smiled and obliged.)

Sure enough, I found myself in that all-too-familiar situation where I was called upon to face up to the repercussions of a seemingly little decision that I had stubbornly made.

Billy Joel knows this all too well and in fact I think he wrote the following verse of his song 'Pressure' for me, especially as Pete stood up to bat in the final innings of the grand final with our previously unbeaten side in a desperate situation with two men out and one run in arrears. Luckily, we had loaded bases. Softballers will tell you, the script couldn't have been that much more dramatic:

Now here you are in the ninth
Two men out and three men on
Nowhere to look but inside
Where we all respond to PRESSURE!

Despite Billy's song annoyingly crawling around my brain like an uninvited relative at Christmas, I heard the team exhorting Pete to keep his eye on the ball. Then, like most coaches when it really matters, I found my mouth shouting out something light-years from profound: *You can do it, Pete! I know you can!*

Peter didn't look at me with his customary H-you're-a-dickhead sideways glance. He just concentrated on the pitcher as the unflappable creep stood on the mound, halting time itself, before bringing his mitt close to his chest in that telltale sign that he is about to hurl the ball at the plate. Pete uncharacteristically chased the pitch and, despite its incredible speed, he vitally connected the bat to ball. Unfortunately the ball went straight to the nimble short-stop who hadn't made an error all game. But when the ball reached the short-stop's glove, as he transferred it to his throwing arm a moment's hesitancy overcame him. Should he take the easy out at home plate or throw it to the nearest base? As each of our three well-drilled base-runners had already left their bases at the *tonk* of Pete's hit, the short-stop chose to play the way he was facing and fired the ball at the first-baseman.

He in fact fired the ball ten miles over the first-baseman's head and off towards Queanbeyan.

But the important thing was that it wouldn't have mattered one iota because Pete, who had pumped his little pistons to oblivion all month at training, would have made it safely to first base anyway. As the ball continued on its merry journey into New South Wales, our second base-runner ran over home plate and emphatically stamped on it. The stands erupted.

Me? I was just relieved. Had Pete struck-out or popped an easy fly, I am not sure how I would have felt. Disappointed. Possibly philosophical. Perhaps postulating that there was nothing to guarantee that a more proficient hitter than Pete would have necessarily middled the ball when the stakes were so high. But as the boys were hoisting Peter above their shoulders, I knew intrinsically I had done the right thing in letting every player in the squad be a part of that grand final. Even if things hadn't gone our way, I knew I had taken the correct path.

I also knew that was easier to say *after* we had won.

So perhaps the next most odious thing a coach has to do in sport, aside from asking someone to take a penalty kick after extra time, is to substitute or drop a player from a side. I will deal with the latter in the following chapter, but it must be said at the outset that, as I get older and more experienced in sport, I get even sicker in the stomach when doing either of these things. I'm often caught stammering and stuttering. I'm left appearing far too apologetic while striving unsuccessfully for sincerity, rationality and logic, and inevitably end up sounding perilously close to a politician or a used-car salesman. Maybe a politician's gutter ruthlessness is what is required when one does this sort of thing. I am often flummoxed with the ease with which some coaches, particularly those in the quest for success at all costs, can ruthlessly ignore kids during important matches and let them only play a token part in a team's achievements – such as keeping the bench temperature comfortably warm.

In the past few years, I have seen myself confronted by the dilemma of substituting, particularly when reaching the highly charged finals of school and national futsal events. My policy has generally been to give everybody some – but not always the *same* – amount of field time, so that all squad members can feel they have played a part, even if it is a small one, in proceedings. This is easier to do in futsal and junior soccer, when you have unlimited substitutions. Yet in sporting codes which allow unrestricted subbing, you sometimes can get sucked into the feeling that you cannot leave your weaker players out there for too long, especially when a handy lead is shortened or an opposition side starts to pull away in a tight match.

Finals situations well may be a slightly different scenario to pool matches or regular competition games where I see no conceivable reason for players not to get (close to) even time. If they are prone to errors, mistakes and colossal whoppers, it is the coach's brief to do all they can to rectify things for the benefit of the individual player as well as the team. Sadly, the easy solution is to simply take them off when they screw up. While the short-term gain is that there is slightly less likelihood of the team suffering for the weaker player's gumbie presence, it is a) hardly a solution which satisfies the *kaizen* brief and b) hardly develops the profound qualities of tolerance, patience and team unity which sport can provide outside and beyond a superficial win. When recently reading sports psychologist Jeffrey Bond's article 'Training Willpower', I was relieved to read that he felt the same way:

> The coach who benches a player who is trying hard every time they make a mistake is only increasing the chance that the athlete will rejoin the game trying even harder to avoid making the next mistake (that is,

increasing the possibility of making mistakes). Is it any wonder that athletes sometimes show inconsistency, lose interest or show a perceived lack of willpower?

When a player quits (a game, a team or a sport) because of their inconsistent form, lack of interest or inspiration, or a feeling of being ostracised, *the entire team loses a significant part of itself.* Especially if the team, along with its coach, hadn't tried all it could to rise above the junior sporting equivalent of Darwinism. It is my belief that a team's success lies intrinsically in how it treats its (seemingly) weakest players.

I noticed my 2005 Coach's Conduct statement for Futsal ACT included the following clause:

* Avoid overplaying the talented players: the just-average need and deserve equal time.

While the same organisation cheekily publishes dispatches encouraging us to do all we can to put the bigger states like New South Wales back into their dark, dingy futsal holes, it is good to see that coaches at the state level are asked to provide equitable time for all participants even at the elite level.

So, getting back to finals. The more aggressive coach would unequivocally state that you put your best team out on the paddock and do all you can to win. The other players would rather, after all, have a winner's trophy than a runners-up one. Unfortunately, this is hogwash. The sad reality that these coaches tend to overlook is that unless players who have been actively involved in the season (or a tournament or round robin's pool fixtures) actually play some active, even tiny, part in a grand final, the plastic premiership trophy becomes even more hollow than it already is (doesn't anyone make decent trophies any more?), eventually gathering dust in a forgotten part of the shelves – and memories – of all the people concerned.

The enigma with sport is that you are never totally sure what an inconsistent player can produce in a pressure-cooker situation. And if they have been with the team for the whole journey, despite the seduction of finals' success, they really deserve to play a part, albeit a small one, in proceedings at the ultimate time.

In a recent schools futsal final, I can remember having two boys on the bench, one extremely anxious and the other keen to get out there. As I wasn't sure how each would react, I gave both a brief stint on the court when we had a two-goal buffer. As it turned out, the anxious player – whom I put out on the court to give my ears a break from his incessant stream of consciousness about nervousness – played with contrasting assurance and poise and followed my match plan to a T; whereas the quietly confident player went out and was overawed by the situation and disregarded every single one of the tactics I had outlined to him pre-match. He consequently created some match winning opportunities – for the opposition.

While it is true that one of these boys possibly disrupted our wellbeing and equilibrium during the final, both left the stadium feeling integrated into the whole finals experience and, more importantly, into the team. The only thing that truly suffered were my tactics. But as Alex Ferguson states in his autobiography, *Managing My Life*,

> Tactics are important but they don't win football matches. Men win football matches. The best teams stand out because they are teams, because the individual members have been so truly integrated that the team functions with a single spirit. There is a constant flow of mutual support among the players, enabling them to feed off the strengths and compensate for weaknesses. They depend on one another, trust one another.

If this is the case with your team when they reach finals or play important games, that they are 'truly integrated' and functioning with a single spirit, then you will achieve the true results you seek, which exist *beyond* scorelines.

In short, if people in your squad are left out of significant experiences, you may well find yourself in possession of a premiership flag or a tournament trophy.

And not have won anything at all.

Training Module 9
How I Learned to Stop Worrying and Love the Bomb

Special delivery – a bomb – were you expecting one?

Inspector Clouseau / Peter Sellers,

The Revenge of the Pink Panther, 1978

My recent experiences as an Under 11 Futsal ACT coach have certainly highlighted my inadequacies when it comes to dropping bombs, particularly on little people. When Under 11s do not make the cut, they have a tendency to disintegrate instantly, creating puddles of tears at their feet while their faces begin to crease inwards as if something behind their nose was sucking their facial features back in towards their brains. Their parents, who have vicariously kicked (or missed) every single ball in every drill at the trials, also start to crinkle up but tend to respond by releasing this energy outwardly, usually by demanding the coach's job.

After trials at a club or state level, I'm often left feeling the need to create a whole new second shadow team in order to give each of these kids whose faces I've caused to implode a bright, new opportunity to shine and grow and somehow negate the need for the selection process in the first place. But I know, in my heart of hearts, that this is all just a vain and desperate fantasy on my part. As Bill Cosby once pointed out, 'I don't know the key to success, but the key to failure is trying to please everybody.' I am, unfortunately prone to wanting to please everybody. A mother at that Under 11 trial made it worse by saying to me, *The boys don't look at it as being dropped by The Coach or The System, George. They look at it as being dropped by you. And that really hurts because they like you so much.* Gee, thanks. I feel a hell of a lot better now, lady.

I asked my fellow Under 11 A coach that year, Darren Pietrzak – who has won more national titles than any members of his teams have seen birthdays – what he felt about the whole selection process blues and he calmly replied to me, *I love it, George. Trying to pick the best team and then making it work at the national level is an exciting feeling.* I said to him it possibly made me feel worse than the imploding kids I had dumped. He pertly responded, *It's life, mate. You sometimes get picked, you sometimes don't. You've got to get used to things not going your way. And then either let it beat you or grow from it.*

He then had the audacity to imply that I was a 'softie'.

Darren proceeded to give me a lecture, with an accompanying video called *Come Fly With Me*, about how Michael Jordan was dropped as a sophomore from his varsity basketball team. Young Michael evidently wasn't ready, at that point of his life, for the rigours of school representative basketball. Motivated by his rejection, he obviously then worked pretty damned hard at shooting hoops and dribbling. After growing a further four inches, he led the Laney Buccaneers to their first ever conference championship two years later, shattering all scoring records along the way. He then went on to become the most famous basketballer that the world had ever seen.

That story made me feel a little better.

It made me recall reading an account by the current National Youth Team's coach Ange Postecoglou in *Our Socceroos* about sitting next to a rejected Youth World Cup player on a plane back to Melbourne. Ange felt uncomfortable, as he had collected the final spot on the team:

> I remember wondering at the time what would become of that player and whether he would stick with it. It turned out that while I only played four times for the senior national team, the guy sitting next to me ended up playing more Socceroo games than anyone else in history, including many as captain. His name was Alex Tobin.

I guess Alex, with 117 appearances in green and gold, like Mikey J, didn't let disappointment become disillusionment. In fact, they both obviously used their rejection as motivation.

As I was driving home, it seemed incredibly evident what I needed to do. I needed to learn how to stop worrying and love the bomb. Hell, if dropped carefully it might release enough energy, inspiration and impetus to create Futsal ACT's answer to Michael Jordan.

The dubious 'team' of kids I have dropped throughout fifteen years of coaching would be quite large. And I remember each and every one of them.

I assume they remember me too.

As a kid, I was often stirred up when dropped from teams. Call me an intense freak if you will, but I can still remember pretty much every coach and director who didn't read my name out after trials and auditions respectively. That I still want, even after all these years, to pour ice down their shirts in the middle of winter or enclose them in an elevator with a rabid St Bernard should give you some idea of the extent of my need for either the Alexander technique, a sound effects CD of some waves breaking on the shore or even a good old fashioned primal scream.

As I recall, my disappointment was more acute when the *process* was either unfair or shonky. As a junior state baseballer in my early teens, I would wait in abject horror during team announcements as the coaches' and managers' sons were instant selections, followed by their clubmates, then supplemented by the more popular players from elsewhere. I was lucky in those formative years that I had an assistant coach by the name of Pat Britten who championed my cause and noticed my efforts to maintain fitness (hell, I stopped smoking at the start of Year 7 for the sake of baseball), spending extra time catching flies, keeping my eye in with the pitching-machine after everyone left, and on top of all that getting much needed external advice on how to improve my suspect throwing action. Yet when Pat left the rep scene, as mentors invariably do, so did my chances of selection in subsequent years. I remember being wickedly thrilled when I heard that my replacement in the Under 15s had played up pretty badly when interstate (rumour had it he took his billet's new car for a joy-ride) and had been forced to return home in disgrace by the new coach halfway through the Nationals. I dreamed up what I was going to say to the coach when he'd eventually call me STD and beg me to rejoin the team. Heck, I'd say something clever like *No thanks, mate!* Perhaps fortunately, the call never came.

Now I'm not usually a quitter, but my disillusionment with the *process* at a time when my hormones were mercilessly poking at my cranky gland, found me quitting baseball unceremoniously a year later. I remember losing the grand final to Pat's team and not being able to look him in the face when it seemed clear I was unable to hit a beached whale with a mallet that day.

I'm sure that Michael Jordan and Alex Tobin would share my confidence in American playwright Paula Vogel's maxim 'Do not believe in opinions of your potential or predictions of your future, or be swayed by the embitterments of the past'. But it is strange, isn't it, how vividly one can recall all these moments of significant disappointment and disillusionment almost as strongly as the day one was dropped. Then revisit those moments, now as a coach, when you see other luckless kids going through the same anguish which *you* have created.

It is a matter of conjecture whether I was in fact good enough to remain in the rep baseball team after two good years. I repaid Pat's faith in Perth in 1980 by tonking the ball all over the park and having a perfect fielding average. (When one plays in the outfield for the ACT this is not an easy thing to achieve, as you are frequently given very difficult fielding demands by meaty batsmen from the larger, meaner states.) Yet being dropped had stayed in my head longer than most incidents, possibly due to the fact that kids have an innate sense of when things are dodgy. They are intuitive little buggers, children, and they tend to know a politician or used-car salesman when they see one. They also have an intrinsic and realistic sense of their own abilities when removed a few kilometres from hype. For instance, when I was dropped from the ACT tennis team after being given a chance to play at the elite level in Albury in my mid-teens, I took it all on the chin because my backhand was as weak as American beer. I knew I didn't have the goods and appreciated the chance to find out if that was in fact the case.

I also appreciated that I'd never represent ACT in tennis again.

So what am I exactly saying here?

I guess, aside from working through my own sense of guilt and betrayal, I am suggesting that each coach must recognise five basic principles. That

   1) *For most kids who trial, that trial is the most*

important thing in the world. Even if it doesn't seem imperative to the child to be picked, it doesn't hurt to approach each triallist assuming that it is. The little buggers sometimes delight in conflicting body language – such as shoulder-shruggy nonchalance and droopy apathy, especially if their parents are nearby – when it really, truly, deeply matters inside. Make sure you have designed your sessions thoroughly so as to give all kids a chance to shine and for you to be more able to clearly decide and differentiate.

2) *Parents are nothing but a hindrance at trials.* Most kids and coaches wish they would vanish somewhere else, like Queanbeyan. Most kids also perform better (at trials) without the baggage of expectation and that sinister, vicarious weight that parents can transpose to them with something as slight as a pensive glance or a small sentence of advice. While responsible for a child's birth, they are not responsible for their selection. Thus, they should go shopping or have a coffee or visit a friend and let the kid be.

3) *Each kid has the potential of a nuclear warhead.* Be aware of this. Each kid could be a Michael Jordan some day. So drop them carefully and thoughtfully. Do not clip their wings as they may make a video asking you to come fly with them in later years when they are rich and famous.

4) *At the very least, give the dumpee the opportunity to know why they were cut. Kids generally need calm,*

rational and logical reasons why they have bombed.
They may not agree with your reasons but it is
worse to allow them to leave a trial with a sense
of injustice, a heightened desire to rage against the
machine and/or a big excuse to wallow in misery
and create further self-pity. Telling them specifically
what to work on in order to have a better chance
at the next trials and maybe even lecturing them
about Michael Jordan which, although possibly
being condescending, will provide more useful food
for thought on the way to the car park. Besides,
they may not slash your car tyres or blow up your
letterbox.

And lastly,

5) When all's said and done, players remember
coaches and managers who have an honest belief in
them, no matter how small the player or how tiny
the belief, and who then stand by that player and
belief, no matter how big the pot of gold may be at
the end of the rainbow or how long it takes to get
there.

Incidentally, I've dedicated this book to three men who
may not have always picked me for their baseball team,
chosen me for a lead role in a play or fully agreed with
how bizarrely I've handled something in or out of the
classroom but all of whom have shown faith in *what I
might become* if I persisted at this thing I had some flair
for. They then gave me the space and assistance to work

hard at it. They hung around and persisted, advised and honestly evaluated. They shared the success and empathised with failure. They loved what they did as a coach, a director and a mentor. They developed rather than destroyed.

This was even after I initially screwed up, spat the dummy and didn't make the grade.

Training Module 10
What Coach Is That?
(A Beginner's Guide to Identifying Coaches in Your Own Backyard)

Identifying birds becomes easier the more time you spend watching them. The first step is to decide what group a bird belongs to, and then to work out which member of the group it is. A field guide is very useful at this stage. Identifying birds is the same as trying to identify anything. For instance, with a piece of fruit it's obvious whether it's an apple, orange or lemon.

John Dengate, *Attracting Birds to your Garden in Australia*, 1977

In 2004, my stage adaptation of *Not Just Footy* opened in Canberra. In the opening sequence, teen actor Jake Fraser and I parodied a range of coaching types which I had been exposed to in over thirty years of being around the game. This scene was always charged with high comic energy and was a popular part of rehearsals, particularly for young Jake. Canadian director Walter

Learning would often make us repeat the scene outside the theatre so that he could a) have a cigarette, b) stock up on food and drink while flirting with waitresses from the nearby café and c) attempt to attract patrons (and waitresses) from the café to the show in the hope of selling a few advance tickets.

His theory worked a treat as the lunchtime crowds would gather in droves to watch a teaser of the play which essentially involved me sending-up a range of coaching styles while Jake represented the poor kids who were subjected to their whims and idiosyncrasies. Sometimes the café patrons would sit for over an hour to watch us at rehearsal. They obviously shared in that guilty universal pleasure of seeing a coach, teacher or well-meaning parent being gently but lovingly mocked. Walter's old world charm and Jake's irritatingly winner cuteness also helped put bums on seats and – hey – I was often left wondering if I was needed at all in the process. *Stop being an asshole, George!* Walter would reproach in his Smokey Bear voice. *And go and learn your god-damned lines so we can save this turkey.*

We did get the 'turkey' off the ground, often to packed houses, so I can suggest little that is negative about our makeshift advertising department. And after every performance, without fail, I would get all the coaches in the audience bailing me up in the foyer and informing me about which category of coach they felt they belonged to. (That was after they called me a great big smart-arse, assuming often incorrectly that I had written the sequence specifically about them.)

So, for your reading pleasure, I invite you to take a little ramble through my botanic garden of coaches – without firearms, please – and see if you can spot any you'd like to feed some seeds to. Or put in a cage.

Species: The Pacers

Identifying characteristics: Pacers flit up and down the sideline following the ball and inevitably end up covering more miles of ground than any of the players on the field. Pacers are constantly crowing out useless bits of information which the team already knows such as COME ON! WE'RE ONE GOAL DOWN!; or helpful advice such as STOP BEING SO SLACK, BOYS! COME ON! LIFT!; or after the other team scores: YOU GOTTA WATCH THAT GUY. I TOLD YOU TO MARK HIM TIGHT! DIDN'T I TELL YOU?; or tactical brilliance such as YOU GOTTA PUSH UP, DEFENCE! PUSH UP! GO ON. PUSH! UP! Pacers' natural habitat is the sideline along which they run parallel to the ball, almost as if they're hypnotised by this little sphere. (They get quite fit from it all as a result.) Pacers think, incorrectly and sometimes sadly, that they have some bearing on matters. Which they don't. After an opposition goal is scored, they become momentarily crestfallen and saunter back to the halfway line with feathers ruffled, more upset than the players. When the opposition has scored a hat-trick of goals against their side, they are often heard winding up their charges with determined phrases like COME ON, BOYS. ONLY FOUR TO WIN. WE CAN DO IT… No one believes them.

Handling tip: Never approach a Pacer during a match or even at the conclusion of a match which they have lost. As a species, they are incredibly hard of hearing under trying circumstances, especially when coming to terms with and/or grasping at excuses for a loss. In fact, they will not listen to you after a win either, as they are too busy displaying their plumage and strutting.

Species: The Statisticians

Identifying characteristics: Statisticians often chirp like they have been nesting on a ledge at the Bureau of Statistics. At half-time, they come into their own and are often heard imparting vital data to their charges such as emphasising the need to score another 2.7 goals to maintain an average of 5 goals per match in light of possession dropping 33.3% (recurring) in the last 26% of the game in which the team only gave a 53% effort utilising 17.2% of its collective brain capacity. In fact, the whole season is presented in terms of a mathematical equation: a team may have to win three of the last five games in order to win the premiership and hence should get out there and inch themselves one-third of the way towards one hundred per cent glory as they wouldn't want to be in the position of having to win two from the last three matches, or, God forbid, three from the last three. Refs, incidentally, aren't free of them either and are frequently informed by the Statistician about the exact number of fouls an opposition player/team has committed throughout a match or passage of play. Refs are regularly questioned how long they are going to let rival players/teams get away with things. Usually passive, refs frequently have a violent urge to kill Statisticians and leave their remains dripping at the doorsteps of relatives.

Handling tip: Statisticians often carry clipboards, expensive multimedia equipment, iPods, palm pilots, calculators and/or portable whiteboards with a pencil case crammed full of non-permanent markers. Stealing any of these items will render the Statistician impotent and hence safe to feed, pet or gently cradle.

Species: Drill Sergeants

Identifying characteristics: These are a highly organised yet ruthlessly bossy species and often have English or Scottish accents. They are obsessed with pre-match warm-up routines (usually developed by Chinese gymnasts) which involve a lot of whistle-blowing, straight lines and frustrated bellowing about kids these days not being focused. Their routines are often broken down into 'phases' designed to increase ball control which they espouse to be 'the essence of football'. Each phase has its own name (like The Dam Buster Sequence) and inevitably concludes with the DS dividing teams into pre-combat simulation units identified by bibs. Often, teams are left feeling too exhausted to actually participate in matches after these intense warm-up routines. DS coaches find creativity, spontaneity and improvisation to be an infernal curse and subsequently have all free kicks (both direct and indirect), corner kicks, goal kicks, throw-ins and post-goal celebrations numbered and intricately choreographed. In short, a swift, merciless clinical wiping out of all pockets of resistance is expected each weekend or there'll be hell to pay (such as a sequence of one hundred sit-ups or a hill sprint next training) for the entire squadron. Drill

Sergeants are, after all, not present at games to make friends.

Handling tip: Handle like a grenade with the pin pulled. Never give advice or suggest modern (that is, post World War II) coaching practice, as what a DS has been doing has obviously worked for fifty years – and for their parents before them – and helped them get through front-line combat and tricky enemy lines. In fact, liken every match to front-line combat and they will be your ally for life.

Species: The Optimists

Identifying characteristics: Annoyingly tame scavengers, Optimists are often heard chirping at their charges to keep their heads up even when they have suffered a 27–0 loss. They often quote from sport literature or Hollywood films in which the underdogs have somehow succeeded against all odds. They irritate everyone involved with the team by genuinely listening to, then clumsily acting upon, *everyone's* a) suggestions on what exactly is going wrong and b) advice on how to go about fixing things. If ever actually winning a game, Optimists will totally blow it by substituting the best player on the field with the least coordinated player on the bench in order 'to keep things fair and equitable'. However, they are a tame, warm-hearted species and are frequently seen to be buying the team Cokes, taking them ten-pin bowling, organising a profit-sapping lamington drive or shouting their charges a rewarding and rejuvenating Happy Meal at McDonald's if the side loses by less than 10.

Handling tip: As an end-of-season present, buy them a copy of the Dalai Lama's *Art of Living*, enrol them in a tai chi course and give them a hamper of fruity herbal teas. Then find a new coach.

Species: The Screamer

Identifying characteristics: This species scream all the time: when reading the team list, thinking out loud, giving a simple instruction, delivering half-time speeches, manifesting their frustration or even when saying thank you to their wife for getting a coffee at half-time. Evolution has totally eradicated the gland which produces the subtlety hormone.

Handling tip: Proceed as if they actually are normal. Their volume is just hot air.

Species: Al Pacino

Identifying characteristics: A dangerous, foul-mouthed species of coach, Al Pacinos are usually linked with organised crime in the neighbourhood (and have an unusually and scary level of devotion to their mothers). They often take their players away from where parents are gathered at half-time so they can a) swear profusely at their charges regardless of age; b) encourage their developing pugilists to engage in 'fist therapy' or to yank the balls of opposition players who are getting the better of them; c) congratulate players who have received yellow or red cards; d) congratulate players who should have received yellow or red cards and got away with it; e) apologise for not teaching the boys enough dirty tricks at training; and f) tell a few yarns about when they were a kid and how tough it was and how tough they are now and how tough this bunch of pussies they are coaching need to become. If a member of Al Pacino's team is injured during a match, they are always told to get up or be wasted.

Handling tip: As in all Hollywood gangster flicks, the Al Pacinos will eventually get their comeuppance, because they have pissed off too many people in their lifetimes.

So do not take out hasty and immediate revenge on their family. Just be patient, as these types will eventually end up being carted away to an unmarked grave someplace.

Species: The Parent/Coach or Parent/Manager

Identifying characteristics: Usually roped in because nobody else wants to do the job or because the parent has a son/daughter in the team, this unfortunate inbred species (while sometimes providing a healthy 'family' tone to a team) is generally too aggressive a creature of prey to have hanging around your training ground. They squawk incessantly about the virtues of their child, often recounting why their child is the best player in the team and regularly boring everyone to tears when outlining the intricate pathway their child is following all the way to the next World Cup. (They often have an accompanying Powerpoint presentation and/or flowcharts as a visual aid.) Regularly found nesting on club and state committees, they make themselves totally indispensable to a particular sporting body, maintaining their dominance over others by having their own company, business or associated corporation sponsor the club or sporting code in question with vast amounts of money. Often, their offspring's minimal talents in controlling and manipulating a ball on the sportsfield are greatly surpassed by their own considerable talent for manipulation and control off the field.

Handling tip: Feed them manure regularly. Make friends with them as soon as possible. Encourage your kids to make friends with their kids, also ASAP.

Species: The Cockatoo

Identifying characteristics: The 'cockie' or whinger-coach is an aberration of the coaching species. They become obsessed with match officials and end up screeching at them more than the players on their team. They know every rule and regulation backwards and are frequently quoting them back at referees, opposition parents or any detractors who have seen things differently – that is, incorrectly. They will always check opposition sides' match cards prior to matches to ensure that opposing teams are not using over-aged or unregistered players. Despite doing this, they will blame over-aged and unregistered players for a loss after the game anyway. An endearing trait of this coaching type is that if your team loses, the cockatoo is likely to blame 'the mongrel referee', 'the blind as a bat' line official (with no discernible understanding of the offside rule), the deplorable state of the pitch, the overriding weather conditions, Saddam Hussein, local government and a general universal lack of empathy, resources and funding for their personal plight. The loss is *never* attributed to the level of coaching the team has or hasn't received from the cockatoo.

Handling tip: Agree with them in public and then impersonate them in the car on the way home and over dinner. Also, deliberately forget to invite them to team or club functions so you can continue with your impersonations in a more public arena.

Species: The Saint

Identifying characteristics: This species rarely has a direct sharehold in the team that s/he coaches. They generally are parents, ex-players or community-minded sports lovers who volunteer their services in order to put back into a sport a little of the good they received from it when they were younger. These coaches stick in the memory longer than most of the other figures from your past. And sometimes, if you're really lucky, you get a saintly coach who is *really* special. Someone whose little sayings or small but significant gestures lift off from the paddocks of the past and stay with you for a lifetime. Someone who shows you ways of making the struggle in small things like sport, and shows that larger things, like life, are well worth working at. Success is rarely what you remember them for, although you invariably succeed in some way because good karma follows this species around. The Saint species knows about *kaizen* intuitively, is rarely perturbed by a loss of any magnitude and can still see positive outcomes in moments of utter despondency. Essentially, it may not be in wins but through *winning moments* where, as a result of your experiences with this type of coach, you find yourself to have developed, evolved, learned and grown more fully as a human being under this person's care and concern.

Handling tip: Bottle and preserve them. Treat them like royalty. And every now and then, without the aid of expensive gifts, lavish media attention or formal, official or ostentatious presentations, tell them they matter.

Training Module 11
Old-fashioned Concepts Like Allegiance and Loyalty

The old principles of a player playing for a club
out of allegiance and loyalty have all but gone out
the window. People now just play for the highest
bidder. The creed seems to be: prostitute yourself,
be disloyal, because the club will be to you after
a couple of bad games. It's an unwholesome
mentality.

Les Murray/Johnny Warren in Andy Harper's
Mr & Mrs Soccer, 2004

I'm often left wondering why representative players
always look so constipated. One would have thought
it was a real achievement to crack into elite circles and
get to play at a high, if not *the* highest, level. So why
the cranky face? Surely, learning a verse of the national
anthem is not that difficult.

Every time I've played or coached against a representative
outfit, they seem on edge, quite theatrically arrogant,
and consider it imperative to prove themselves by being

overly aggressive or flashy. It's like the constipation has detrimentally affected not only their cranky-pants faces but their fluidity on the pitch as well. I would conjecture that sport becomes even harder to enjoy at elite levels unless you are winning. So, for reasons already outlined, most taking a shot at greatness are heading for some sort of disillusionment. They certainly get my sympathy, as it is a long way to the top if you wanna rock'n'roll.

But I also wonder if, at a more profound level, the process which they have had to undergo to break into that illustrious circle has taken some sort of toll. It does not get any easier to get noticed for this thing that you love, the higher up the tree you climb. As Irish international Tony Cascarino recalls as a junior trialling at Charlton Athletic,

> When the moment arrived, and I presented myself for the audition, the disillusion was crushing. 'Why have they asked so many other kids? Isn't this supposed to be about me?' A year later it was the same story at Arsenal, when I was invited along to play in one of five consecutive games. Over one hundred kids were called; a handful were chosen. We were like peas on a conveyor belt.

Coming to grips with the shift from being a big fish in a small pond to something the complete opposite, is one tough hurdle for a young representative's ego to overcome. From being the focus of attention to having to once again *make yourself* the centre of attention is no easy step. Especially when you have been told how special you are from an early age by adults in the know.

You have to make tough calls when you are gifted. As the adult world works out how to use your talents – and in doing so impinges on your innocence – there are a myriad of issues for a young person to sort though. On top of having to train very hard, watching your diet and sacrificing afternoons at the movies, you are called upon to be occasionally ruthless to your peers, oppositions and old clubs; the value (or use) of past friendships, partnerships and allegiances are unmercifully questioned; the past seems necessarily discarded in order to move up the ladder to superstardom; and loyalty, of any sorts, becomes a forgotten virtue. Most parents would not dream of demanding this of their children – unless it is disguised as sport.

These tough calls for young people invariably come at important stages in their mental and physical development, and they tend to come all at once. My fear, being blunt, is that it costs them a little of their soul and a lot of their innocence. Obviously, if you end up representing your country at a national or international level, it is generally considered worth sacrificing that small piece of yourself, but what about the thousands if not tens of thousands who simply do not make the grade? What about the discarded peas on the conveyor belt? In *Head to Head*, the one-time Dutch International Jaap Stam unequivocally lamented,

> I feel so sorry for the young players being ushered into the academy system today, and I do mean young. Football clubs are looking for talented kids aged six and seven, then putting them on an assembly line and mapping out their whole life for them. They are told how to play, what to eat, where to go, and when to sleep. They don't have their youth any more. They are missing out on something that can't be given back at a later date, something that should be innocently enjoyed.

As I watch an ever-increasing number of parents of junior players branded as being 'elite' shopping around for the assembly line which best serves their wants and needs, the more I think these clowns need a big slap with a rubber chicken.

It is at times almost laughable if not ludicrous watching these parents-from-hell (we call them 'theatre-parents' in the arts) who play at being Bernie Mandic. They measure up the offers from rival local clubs; caress the material of the prospective playing strip to make sure it is silky, looks flashy and makes them purr; analyse various development programs (which are pompously labelled as 'academies' these days); and create intense migraines for themselves and their children in attempting to ascertain what exactly is the best pathway for their seven-year-old to follow in order to roll on into the representative sphere. The innocent side of life for these kids, as Stam suggests, disappears as quickly as their childhood or the time it takes to scribble a signature on a piece of paper. As childhood innocence tends to be something idyllic, retrospectively treasured by the future adult, it is hardly of any immediate concern or value when measured up against the attraction of possible stardom. And wealth.

My initial response to all this is threefold. Firstly, doesn't it worry anyone else that Bernie Mandic's name is synonymous with Harry Kewell's? (We do not know the name of Russell Crowe's agent and he is comparably more famous/infamous.) In soccer, perhaps more so than most sports, agents are better known than the majority of the players, particularly as their product moves around from club to club while they drive an uncompromising bargain and take a huge cut. But more importantly, doesn't it worry anyone else that parents of seven-year-olds are starting to behave like them?

Secondly, don't be fooled by the term 'academy', its loose terminology not necessarily referring to an austere building with marble pillars but rather to the patch of grass between some nifty, bright-orange witches' hats on an oval anywhere in your home town. Nearly every club has one. It is sometimes just an elaborate disguise designed to fool the unwary that a club or individuals are concerned with some ill-informed notion of development. George Best certainly is intolerant of them. After sending his son Calum to a 'School of Excellence', he proclaimed,

> My advice is that if you come across a boy with natural talent keep him as far away as possible from these people and these schools as they will surely blunt everything he has and fill his head up with shit. Tell him to get down the park and keep playing, playing and playing and he will learn, learn and learn. There is no better way.

While most would agree that you can manufacture a degree of skill by running around a lot of witches' hats, poles and hoops like some performing monkey, professionals like George Best, Tony Cascarino and Jaap Stam have suggested that the academies need to do more with their chimps. Academies are rarely concerned with what Aussie Rules coach Stan Alves identifies as 'those spiritual human qualities that could not be manufactured, qualities such as inner strength and determination'. Issues of mental wellbeing, particularly involving talented but fragile young players, are too often solved by demanding a set of push-ups or another hour with the hats, hoops and poles. (By the way, you can get a set of four witches' hats for under ten bucks these days and start your own

Academy with Calum Best.) You cannot buy inner strength and determination.

Thirdly, why exactly don't these club bargain-shoppers just stay put at the club they originated from? It is usually close in proximity to those significant places where the seven-year-old happily runs, skips and jumps with his childhood friends. In staying put, the kid doesn't need to reinvent himself all the time, lose his/her sense of identity due to constant change and mist-up his childhood memories. Why not remain where you are? Because our modern professional so-called 'role models' generally seem to advocate that a transient nature is a good thing? Don't worry about lasting relationships with people, clubs and larger bodies. Hey, if you want to succeed, you gotta keep *moving*. The sacrifice is only some stability, a bit of childhood innocence and annoying old friends.

As Cascarino tersely said about the modern game, 'Here today – gone tomorrow – we make many acquaintances but few friends.'

I think the whole aesthetic of belonging to a club is corrosive.

As is obvious, I blame those over-paid footballinaires for setting a bad example. While what these super-tarts do on a personal level concerns me very little (in fact, the soapie that is the Beckhams interests me less than an episode of *Desperate Housewives*) the examples these numbskulls with a lot of money are setting for young people and, far worse, some foolhardy and impressionable parents, frequently unsettles me.

You hear, less and less often these days, about players such as Matt Le Tissier, the stylish Southampton striker who played out his career at his lowly dockside club which struggled to avoid relegation most years. His resistance to lures from rival clubs when he was at his peak and his club's relatively sensitive treatment of their superstar when his limbs started to pack it in, are worthy of mention here. He was awarded the Freedom of Southampton in 2002 as most locals felt that there would not have been a St Mary's stadium and an existing Premier League outfit were it not for his 209 goals across 540 appearances (462 starts). As the webmaster of Matt. LeTissier.com points out to the uninitiated,

> Le Tissier represents something that has been lost in the modern game: loyalty. Despite several opportunities to move to more successful clubs during his career, Le Tissier resisted, staying with the club that had given him his break in football, his beloved Southampton. Some say this shows a lack of ambition, but surely the

challenge was far greater at Southampton. Can you actually imagine it being harder to score in a team consisting of mostly international players than in a typical Southampton side from the 1990s? I certainly can't.

It's hard to read things like this and not hope that Matt is enjoying his Freedom of Southampton gratefully. It is getting harder these days to find superstars who have played for over fifteen years at *any* club. One wonders what Le Tissier makes of the modern trend to shop around for clubs in order to attract that extra-million or ten for the coffers?

There can be very good reasons to switch clubs. For instance, as a player and now as a teacher at a private school, I've witnessed first-hand the tough choice gifted players have to make when changing schools means they may have to change teams. Reasons for the change should not be success-oriented and should focus more on what is best for the child in a holistic sense (that is, happiness beyond the sportsfield). And changes should not occur whenever a whimsical need or niggle arises.

As a schoolteacher, I am often bemused by parents who almost annually displace their child from one school to the other, complaining that the previous institution 'did nothing for their child'. I often wonder at what point the parent asks what exactly they (or their child for that matter) is exactly doing *or has done* for the institution they are pooh-poohing. The sad reality is that the child who is getting tussled, tossed and transplanted from one joint to another isn't getting sufficient time to a) work out whether they belong; b) establish any meaningful relationships which would then make them feel they belonged; c) give the place a chance to do something for them; or, more tellingly, d) give *them* a chance to do something *for the place* and in doing so provide them with a feeling that they not only belong but are a part of (as opposed to apart from) the institution.

Soccer clubs aren't all that different from schools in this regard. While it is a given that some soccer clubs, like schools, need to lift their game for various reasons, over time you tend to get as reasonable a percentage of good teachers / coaches as bad ones. And let's face it, you will get bad lecturers, bosses and taxi drivers throughout your life and at some point you will have to learn how to deal with them. I'm not sure that a) hastily skipping a lecture or recklessly changing courses; b) telling the boss where to stick it and quitting your job; or c) stepping out of a moving cab in peak hour are always the wisest decisions to make before you have thoroughly assessed the situation and given something a chance.

One often needs to remind lost, indecisive parents of gifted but constipated young players to stop and take stock of things before leaving a club perceived by them to be 'not up to scratch'. As they are usually living quite vicariously through their children, these parents may have possibly lost sight of the fact that 'elite' is a relative term when you come from a pimple on the face of the planet.

But as more and more of a poor example is being set by our professionals, who change clubs as quickly as their football-boot brands, underwear and nannies, I'm not convinced that things will alter much this century. Particularly in Europe where a) a high percentage of Australian wannabes go; b) where clubs such as the infamous G14 become 'family' in the Mafia sense; and c) where the bigger clubs driven by the dollar, stock market and boardroom insist that *Their Players* should place club before their family, country and soul. It is no small wonder that the Australian kids dreaming of superstardom are starting to conclude that allegiance and loyalty are old-fashioned concepts, and that disregarding them is a necessary evil if you want to get to the top. So now when a young person goes 'clubbing', it means more than just social infidelity.

I'm not sure it's a wise thing for parents to want *over and above everything else* their kids to be the next Harry Kewell playing in the Premier League. As Neil Montagnana Wallace reminds us in *Our Socceroos*,

All told, FIFA report 250 million people playing organised football – one in every twenty-five people on the planet. Even though many of those 250 million players may dream of life in the big time, playing at the pinnacle of their sport, it is a vast understatement to say most of them will not experience it. For example, there are only 220 players in any given round of the English Premier League, and if you try to figure that out as a percentage of people playing the game worldwide, it's enough to send your calculator haywire.

So I did just that. And my smoking calculator came up with the figure that 0.0000088% (recurring) of the soccer-playing population get to play Premier League on any given weekend. True, if you want to play in the lower leagues, you can remove a few noughts. No wonder the reps look constipated. So you can imagine how the level of constipation that the remaining 99.9% (rounded-off) must feel. Not great odds for happiness or success. As Dutch defender Jaap Stam asked in his book *Head to Head*,

What about the ones who are considered not quite good enough? How would you feel after giving up so much to chase a dream that never came true? It would be so hard to take and, unfortunately, too many youngsters are left to face a painful reality because their hopes have been built up by a one-way system that is suiting the clubs but failing the individuals.

The North Pole is a noble thing to travel to. Far be it for me to tell anyone not to chase their dreams, even if the odds are against you. But it doesn't hurt *to be aware of the rates of success in getting to the heights of your future vocation and how cold it can be if you get there.* Or to be ready for how painful it actually can be to plummet and splatter after attempting to scale these dizzy heights. So as a parent, while you're watching your kid juggling in the backyard or through the cones at his/her academy, it probably wouldn't hurt to keep it all in some kind of healthy perspective.

And what if they don't make the grade?

Former Australian representative Danny Moulis recently commented to me that 'the darker side of a football dream is that it can transform into a nightmare'. As already hinted, representative and academy programs have a duty to better counsel players whose dreams have disintegrated into nightmare. They need to provide kids and parents with early warnings. Then gently but honestly provide rational and thorough reasoning for removing a pea from the conveyor belt. And then possibly follow it up further to ensure that support networks are in place so that a disillusioned pea can effectively rebound and/or experience a less painful closure of sorts. Sadly, most junior representative outfits across many sports just read out a list of names at the end of trainings and/or send out an email omitting a player's name from a list.

Not good enough.

You gotta be in it to win it, sure, but I'd personally prefer to see my kids working just as hard at developing – alongside their sporting skills – decent life habits such as mowing lawns for grannies, being nice to their friends and occasionally working on a charitable venture like door-knocking, selling bandanas for CanTeen or starting up a branch of the Oak Tree Foundation to help the underprivileged. While Harry Kewell apparently played a blinder for Liverpool on this day of writing, an article about his inconsistent form at Anfield totally eclipsed Hugh Evans being awarded the title of World Youth Person of the Year 2004 – which actually happened today as well. Hugh, who appears to be spending most of his relatively short life (thus far) making the world a better place for the poor through his Oak Tree Foundation, is relegated to the back pages, much as Southampton have been relegated from the Premier League this year.

You have to applaud former England international David Platt, who stated in his autobiography that 'It is more important to be judged as a person than a player'. As a member of the elite group of Australians to have played in the final rounds of the World Cup, Harry Williams echoed this sentiment when he remarked in *Our Socceroos*, 'In the end, it is just a sport and I am not sure that people should be remembered for being good at a sport.' This sort of message should be upheld and promoted by parents, mentors and schools just as heavily as their trophy cabinets. Besides, it is easier to break into Red Cross door-knocking, start a branch of the Oak Tree Foundation at your school, visit the nursing home, mow for gran and other such charitable concerns than it is to break into professional football circles. It's just harder to get *noticed*! (Almost as hard as getting spotted by a talent scout at one of five consecutive games involving over a hundred children.) But then anything not involving fame, money and success seems to hold less sway with most modern adolescents. As Christopher Bantick lamented in an article in *The Canberra Times* entitled 'Australia's Forgotten Achievers',

> Schools have a responsibility to give heroes other than sporting identities more classroom time. A place to start is with Nobel laureates. Until children, and their parents, can move beyond Ian Thorpe, Adam Gilchrist, James Hird and others, then Australia's heroes will

continue to be defined by sport rather than anything else. We are all the poorer for believing that ignorance is bliss.

In my earlier book, *Not Just Footy*, I touched on the need for adolescents to have real heroes, as well as those who are larger-than-life. Complementing this, I also think that adolescents need *real-life endeavours* (as opposed to Play Station and sporting academies) to balance out the more pie-in-the-sky, dreamy and lofty hopes and aspirations that they or their parents might have. It may seem ridiculous, but I guess I am advocating that a sporting team should do some charity work together. In doing so, they will connect better not only with each other both on and off the field but with their wider community. They will end up the better for it, as charitable work enhances a desire for improvement, selflessness, commitment, hard work and team play over and above the immediate phase of play or short-term gains. As Hugh Evans points out in his book *Stone of the Mountain,*

> ...a sense of community connection seems particularly hard for young people in Australia to achieve... It seems evident that our society prefers the faster fix and not the long-term investment.

Sound familiar?

So I encourage all representative players – if not all adolescents per se – to take Hugh's or my advice and

139

be like the Canberra Raiders and go play with kiddies in hospitals, visit the elderly in a nursing home or raise some money for a charity *as well as* for your overseas trip or silky representative tracksuit. Get your team to sponsor a tsunami orphan and think beyond the 4-4-2. Tracksuits will fade and formations will fail, but investments made beyond oneself do not disappear as easily. You may then be even more susceptible to looking beyond results and into the heart of things. You may recognise that the world exists beyond the dimensions of a soccer pitch. Or four witches' hats.

That way you will unclog your humanity and feel a little better about yourself even if things go awry in your sporting life.

I guess getting this sort of unusual philosophy heard with any conviction in a nation that is getting increasingly expectant of (sporting) world domination is about as likely as my SYCBSOOAL (Save Your Club By Standing Out On a Limb) Academy opening its four witches' hats to a membership of millions.

I hear of the increase in 'superteams' in junior leagues, where the best players congregate at one club, attracting the best coaches – generally those with the best appetite for winning – to best serve their own needs. Yawn. Somebody really needs to call the best (sic) control. This has been going on since cavemen kicked boulders between the legs of woolly mammoths.

Then I hear that the best way to counter all this is to have representative teams playing in club competitions (albeit playing in an older age grouping) and how this is also 'best' for everyone concerned. As no major research has been done in this area that I am aware of, I will not start debating this too much here. Capital Football's Academy Program is trialling this initiative as I write and I trust that they will evaluate it thoroughly, professionally and neutrally and get back to me.

However, I will say two things here.

Firstly, am I the only person who thinks there is something unwise and possibly unethical with a bunch of parents cheering 'Go ACT!' (state) against a struggling bunch of kids from a local outfit (club)? I know if I was a parent of an ACT player I wouldn't feel too great about cheering vociferously for my son / daughter's team given their obvious advantages. Hell, I would almost want to cheer for the *opposition*.

Secondly, I do think it's a great big shame that some of these rep players may never know what it's like to have played for a club in their teens (that is, a 'club' unencumbered with representative agendas) – all during a crucial time of their lives when they learn about the real value of stability in lasting friendships, relationships and other such vital things. Again, I am not sure I would want to encourage my kids to regularly shop around for what best serves their *immediate* needs. I can see some problems inherent in that philosophy.

I also hope that any representative program accounts *just as much for its failures as its successes* and looks after those unsuccessful kids who have made sacrifices for no apparent gains. You hear about the two or three who make the national or international grade constantly, but rarely about the hundreds who do not. And where do they exactly end up? (Back at the discarded club perhaps?) My cynical side suspects that they are dropped from these super-dooper elite sport programs with a 'Thanks anyway' and a 'Welcome to the real world, kiddo'. Now, if a teacher took that attitude to a failing student, they would get hung, drawn and quartered.

The elite coach just accepts the next intake.

So that brings us back to the clubs. I recognise that clubs are imperfect beasts and there may be very good reasons for people to switch 'em occasionally. So I may be standing out on a limb here, but I will still grab stubbornly a hold of the swaying branches around me and state that a Le Tissierian philosophy of 'staying put' with a club and nurturing its strengths and ironing out its weaknesses – a process which takes time and hard work – will allow the average players to develop far more lasting qualities in their sporting life and their real life.

Friendships made become less superficial and longer-lasting; an understanding and belief in the benefit of seeing things through to completion becomes a vital creed; the intrinsic worth of remaining loyal against the seduction of trend, fashion and success allows one to develop into a more genuine human being; the rock of allegiance will provide a stronghold in the centre of life's shifting sands; working with people of various abilities must bring out leadership qualities, where inspiration can become a mutual experience; and, in the end, it puts the onus back on players to assume (even some) responsibility for their own futures and their own environments simultaneously. You need to *stay somewhere long enough* for these things to occur.

At the very least, when things get tough, parents need to help their kids consider the pros and cons, complexities and sensitivities of an issue more fully before easy abandonment. There is no need to emulate footballinaires or listen to myopic experts in this regard.

I am not sure if I've been too unsympathetically tough on parents and coaches who only want the best for their kids, but as an axe-murderer states in DBC Pierre's 2003 Booker Prize winner, *Vernon God Little,* 'You (are) stuck in the snakepit of human wants, wants frustrated and calcified into *needs,* achin' and raw.' So before you make that move, consider the wood for the trees. The calcified wants from the needs. You may ache a little less.

Matt Le Tissier scored forty-nine out of fifty penalties in his Premier League career. That takes balls of steel and equal amounts of wisdom and craftiness. I like to think that if Matt was given the Freedom of the City in Canberra, he would be found standing up on the tree where the SYCBSOOAL Academy meets, along with me, maybe clinging for dear life. But still high enough to cheer for the local club side as they take on the state's best. Or some other concocted superteam.

Given a choice, dear reader, if I was a junior league kiddie or junior league mummy and daddy or even a junior league suit, I would follow Matt Le Tissier's example.

And hang around with my club for a year or fifteen.

My father made a windmill full of friends through soccer in the 1930s in Holland.
(Dad was goalkeeper, front row, third from the left.)
This loose 'kind of marriage of people' stayed friends for life.

The ACT Under 13 Baseball side of 1980 in Perth for the National Junior Baseball
Championships. I decided to show my better side.

Sitting with my baseball mentor Pat Britten whose son/batboy, Anthony, is checking on the state of my dislocated elbow – the result of wayward Queensland pitching.

My first and last softball side: the Radford First IX, 1997.
My friend Barry left them, undefeated, in my hands when he got posted to Yeppoon.
His simple parting instruction was to win the premiership and send him a trophy.
Without compromising our 'give-everyone-a-go' mentality, we did both.

Mum and I at my 30th birthday party in 1997. Jeane sure knew something and taught me more about team spirit than the mighty KISS Army.

Mum always made sure that supporters of both teams would have little negative to say by putting a hot drink in their hands.

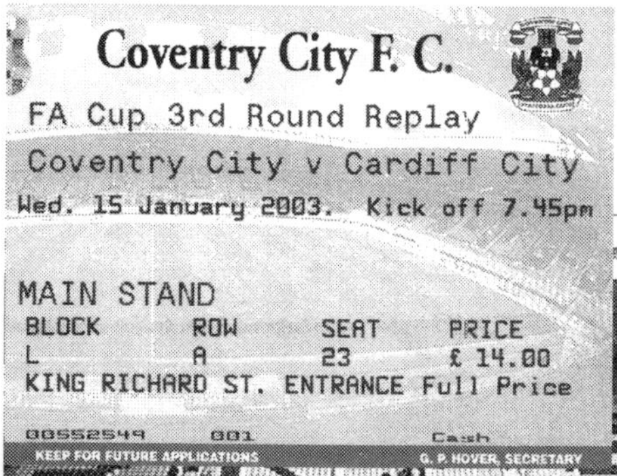

The ticket purchased for the scariest sporting event I have ever attended: Coventry vs Cardiff, 15/1/2003.

Coventry City F. C.

FA Cup 3rd Round Replay
Coventry City v Cardiff City
Wed. 15 January 2003. Kick off 7.45pm

MAIN STAND
BLOCK   ROW   SEAT   PRICE
L   A   23   £ 14.00
KING RICHARD ST. ENTRANCE Full Price

00552549   001   Cash
KEEP FOR FUTURE APPLICATIONS   G. P. HOVER, SECRETARY

At Highfield Road, my beloved Coventry City's home turf, in quieter times.

In 2001, I found myself in Loreto, Italy, where the Adriatic Sea air helped me collect some thoughts about football and life.

The Black Madonna statue, held within the Sanctuario della Santa Casa, didn't produce too many miracles when I was there.

The luckless Bill Turner Squad of 2001. This side had an unusually high proportion of Australian representatives including Kaz Patafta (Soccer), Nick Norton (Softball), James Bennett (Australian Rules) and Murray Clapham and Kevin Room (Futsal). As a whole, the squad missed out on a semi-final spot in the Cup because they missed penalties. Since that day, I have vowed to erase this diabolical practice from soccer for good...

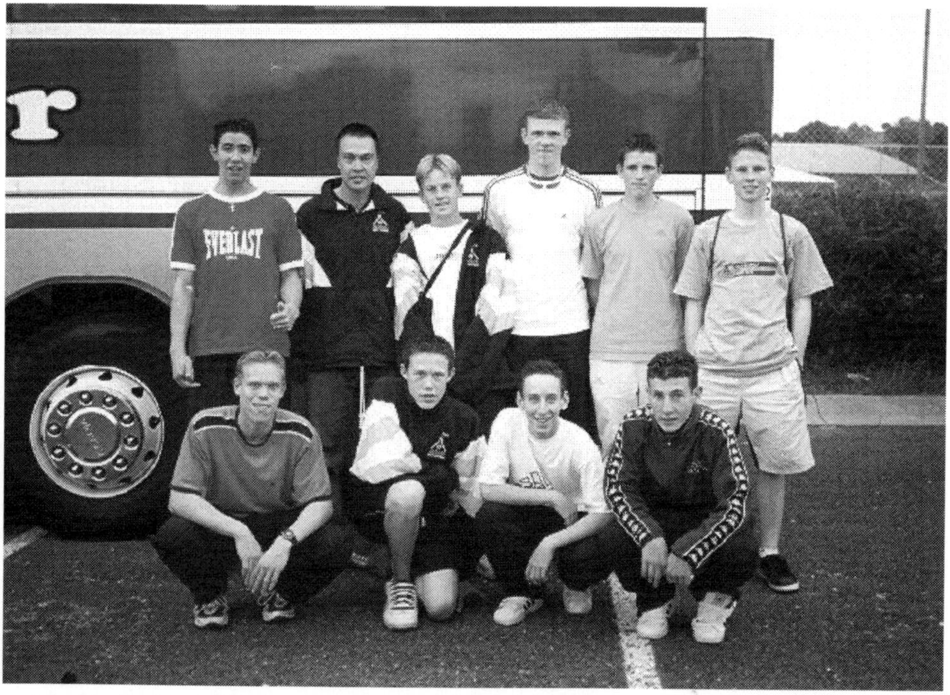

The Under 16 ACT Blues, September 2002, about to return home from the National Futsal Championships in Albury (and still waiting for the cheerleaders). These lovable rogues succeeded significantly without ever winning.

The Ladies' Men, all gelled and ready for action in the hotel prior to the 2003 Brisbane Schools Championships for Futsal. The squad was: Wozza, Tuckers, H, Al, Rhys, Aidan, Sundo and 'Cheap Points' Charlie.

In between fixtures at Cornubia Sports Complex, The Ladies' Men released tension by 'training' in the kids' playground.

The Ladies' Men, Movie World, September 2003. Winning the championship was sweet, but the Lethal Weapon ride proved a bigger challenge, especially for Charlie.

Photos taken during the stage adaptation of Not Just Footy *(HMT, June 2004),*
featuring Jake Fraser as little George and me as my father.
Dad's gentle, unassuming instruction tended to work the best with George Jr, while
goal-side lectures never went down quite as well.

Fun was always had at training,
something desperately missing from the modern coaching handbooks.
Playing air-guitar to KISS songs kept me fitter than most throughout the 70s.

I always figure the best way to talk to players is like you've known 'em for years.

John Huitker (and me).

Jann Lennard – who always appears at important times along the Soccer Time & Space Continuum – with her father Jack, a former soccer Olyroo of 1956. Both Jann and I coach to give back to sport a little of what our unforgettable fathers gave to us.

The author getting down to the correct level to talk with the Radford Taipans in Brisbane during the 2004 National Schools Futsal Championships.

Following in The Ladies' Men's footsteps, the Radford Taipans took out the National School's title.

The ACT Under 12 Colts saluted to the sun at the 2005 Futsal Nationals in Canberra, perhaps treating sport with the seriousness it deserves.

*It doesn't hurt to find some good role models somewhere.
Two important mentors in my life have been Canadian theatre director Walter Learning (left) and the Best Deputy Principal in the World, John Leyshon (right).*

Part Two
Match Reports

12: Heads

Coaching the Blues

Two sides of the coin to choose from
Two sides of the coin they are mine
Two sides of the coins, I'm getting weary
Which one should I choose – I need time

Ace Frehley, Two Sides of The Coin, 1980

Indoor fireworks can still burn your fingers.

Elvis Costello, Indoor Fireworks, 1986

Without any warning, he lifted the branch he had ripped from a defenceless tree and smashed it into the service station bin in one, short random assault. The lid caved in significantly under the force of the blow, becoming V-shaped in the process. The metallic cylinder beneath creased contritely inward and the crash of impact reverberated for what seemed like the length of the empty Hume Highway. Birds shotgunned from a line of eucalypts in the adjacent parkland and my team, ever slow in reaction time, swung around at the explosive sound with a flummoxed *whathehellwasthat?* inquiry on each of their pimply faces.

It was still light at 7.00 p.m. and the idea was that the boys and I would take a reflective post-dinner perambulation around this strange, new environment in which we were a visiting state futsal team. *Let's soak up the ambience,* I had said. *Acclimatise. Something you should do before any game.* Find some focus and peace and unity before the hubbub and clamour and sheer intensity of a screaming sports hall, where its unrelenting din would inevitably distract, dull and drown out even the most soulful whimper of any deeper, spiritual, sporting voice. The idea was to simply walk, quietly (that is, without talking, as the Side of Silence Special XI play), and to think about what we would do, both as individuals and as a team and as representatives of state when it all counted on the national stage in under twenty-four hours.

It was probably the silence that threatened them.

Sixteen-year-olds are suspicious of it and like to fill gaps in the noise with the angst of LA's machine-gun rap-prophets. With whining. Or with farts. And perhaps it was just the plain cuteness of Albury birds, warbling a twilight song before nightfall that really got on their tits. Whatever the case, it was too much for one.

Smash!

Why the hell did you do that, Morto?

I dunno.

With a penitent look, he tried to straighten the lid, which would now only balance precariously on top of the buckled garbo. His teammates scanned the streets for signs of an Albury PD Blue swat team while the coach took in very deep breaths. (This would not be the first time these boys would exasperate him.)

Honestly, Morto, why in God's name did you do that? I repeated.

Pause.

I really don't know. I just felt like whacking somethin'. I feel a bit intense about tomorrow and I just lost my cool...

I looked at him with mild disappointment, recapping in my mind Alex Ferguson's claim that former Chelsea hothead Dennis Wise could start a fight in an empty room. Nothing new here then.

I said, *If you can't control yourself while taking a stroll down the street, what hope have you got of controlling yourself on the pitch in the heat of the moment?*

Standard response: *I dunno.*

Well, maybe you should spend a bit of time thinking about it.

And maybe I needed to spend a bit of time rethinking why the hell I was here in the first place. David Byrne's anxious, trembling voice now began squawking edgily in my head…

My God. How did I get here?

My friend Jann, whose presence indicated that something profound was going to happen once again along the STAS (Soccer Time and Space) continuum, asked me if I would like to coach an ACT Futsal team in 2002. I was coaching an Under 15 group from my present Radford outdoor side called Lotus (now there's a name with connotation), who played the indoor game for fun over summer and were making an impact on the local competition. While I enjoyed a lot of things about indoor soccer, reading the game was as bewildering to me as reading Samuel Beckett. And since I was a kid, I have always been prone to say 'yes' when requested to do something unusual and/or difficult, particularly in regard to sport. As Christopher Lasch once wrote,

> Games simultaneously satisfy the need for free fantasy and the search for gratuitous difficulty; they combine childlike exuberance with deliberately created complications.

This exuberant, childlike need to marry fantasy and complexity off against each other pretty much governs all my hobbies and is what found me saying 'yes' immediately to Jann. I had also assumed that I would coach her youngest son, Murray, who was in this particular age group. I thought Murray to be a brilliant kid because his two hobbies were also soccer and the theatre, so he would have an inherent understanding of the delightful creative tension caused by combining imagination and obstacles.

As I was to find out, ACT places two sides into each age level for The Nationals, one called ACT Gold, the other ACT Blue. I was already pretty blown away by the creativity in Futsal ACT's naming policy and hoped they'd be far too busy making up other wacky team names to notice that I didn't have any formal futsal coaching qualifications. As Bill Shankly is often quoted as saying, 'Football is a simple game based on the giving and taking of passes, of controlling the ball and of making yourself available to receive a pass. It is terribly simple.' So I figured if such a philosophy worked for Shankly, I could adopt a similar one for my inaugural bout as a state coach at anything.

I attended what was to be the final Under 16 trial and watched as Chris D'Silva, the Gold coach, ran the lads through a sequence of drills (which made little sense to me) and the regulation scratch match before finally announcing his side, which included Murray. Chris told the remaining players – and there were only half a dozen – not to despair, as I would be taking them to Albury as The Blues, this being the second-string Under 16 side. The boys looked up at me as if I was wearing a fig leaf and then asked when the next training was to be, where we would train and whether we would play 'rotation'.

I told them I'd get back to 'em. I always say that when caught off-guard.

I hitched a ride home with Jann and was tossing up whether now to stay on and coach the side as, firstly, I knew even less about futsal after that trial than I did before it and, secondly, I assumed the only reason Jann wanted me to coach was to make sure Murray got to play at the Nationals. Yet here was a chance for me to try to coach – at a representative level – a bunch of kids I didn't know at a sport I also knew nothing about. The appeal was undeniable.

I informed Jann I'd be borrowing some of her futsal coaching books, told Murray I was disappointed not to be coaching him (and he diplomatically said that the feeling was mutual) and then said to nobody in particular, *What the hell does 'rotation' mean?*

For the uninitiated, futsal is a form of indoor soccer which is starting to get the recognition it deserves in this country. The name 'futsal' comes from the merging of the Spanish/Portuguese words for football (futbol or futebol) and the French or Spanish word for 'indoor' (salon or sala). In 1989, FIFA officially identified the name 'futsal' to represent all indoor soccer and five-a-side activities. My friends often look at me as if I've mentioned a fungal disease when I use this term, but so be it.

It was the Canadians who actually recorded the first game of indoor soccer in 1854, but a version closer to the modern game was developed by Juan Carlos Ceriani for YMCAs in Uruguay in 1930. This was the same year that Uruguay hosted the first FIFA World Cup, so one must never play down this country's contribution to the development of football, even though they ruined our chances of playing in the last outdoor World Cup. Ceriani, fed up with rain getting in the way of his practices and fixtures, moved the game indoors, developed, defined and laid out a set of rules, and in no time at all the game's popularity had expanded across South America and over to Europe.

A hybrid of the game was being played in Brazilian streets around this time and no doubt the Brazilians would argue that this was the true origin of the game which Ceriani formalised. While the first leagues of the sport appeared in Brazil, it was Paraguay that won the inaugural international futsal series when it took out the South American Championship in 1965. This really got up Brazil's goat and they went on to win the next six. The first World Championship was held in 1982 in Sao Paolo and Brazil took home-court advantage to win the inaugural and subsequent titles, although Paraguay refused to remain unnoticed in futsal circles by winning the third in Australia in 1989. Last year in Taipei, Spain emerged as the new futsal powerhouse by beating the European Champions, Italy, 2–1 to take the World Champions' title for the second time in a row. Let's all have a paella to celebrate.

As with Uruguay, YMCAs must be happening places because it was at the Revesby YMCA in 1972 that Dawn Gilligan introduced the game to Australia, again after a wet soccer season. (This sport owes a lot to rainfall.) The game filtered down to Canberra where Futsal ACT was inevitably formed in 1985. Unlike the outdoor game, Australian indoor teams have featured in all five FIFA Futsal World Cups held in the Netherlands, Hong Kong, Spain, Guatemala and Chinese Taipei, but in 2004 the futsaloos (that's my wacky term – feel free to use it) returned from Taipei without a single point from their round matches. 2002 was the year when unknown coach George Huitker first took charge of the ACT Under 16 Blues side without realising and knowing anything written in the last four paragraphs.

In *Sheilas, Wogs and Poofters,* Johnny Warren prophesies that futsal will become one of the great entertainment sports of the twenty-first century and believes that the game plays a big part in Brazil's success in outdoor football, producing superstars such as Ronaldo and Romario. In one of his many trips to Brazil, Warren observed,

> ...that the young players were literally forced into using the proper kicking technique and playing with their heads up by the very nature of the game. Everyone was constantly in motion, making runs to support their teammates. I began to appreciate that all the amazing skills of the senior Brazilian players, all their wonderful dribbles and feints, come from having to play pressure games when they are young in an area restricted in space. If they can't dribble and find their own solution to the limited space in futsal they simply don't survive as a player.

Slow and scant recognition of the worth of the game has retarded its growth throughout its brief history in Australia, and it is pleasing to see most states eventually heeding a recent FIFA directive to embrace the game and recognise it as an imperative part of development of football in general. Capital Football, at the time of writing, was in the process of incorporating Futsal ACT under its wing, while the Mitchell Report commissioned by the former Soccer Canberra in 2004 highlighted the NSW Premier Soccer 2003 Task Force Report's call for the intrinsic value of futsal to be better recognised and utilised for the benefit of the outdoor game. While recognising that a direct mimic of Brazil's football culture is difficult, given the contrasting demographics of our countries, both reports concur that it would be a little silly, stubborn and stupid not to recognise the results of one of the best soccering countries on the planet. As the Mitchell Report points out,

> Many past and current Brazilian star players including Rivelino, Eder, Zico, Leonardo, Ronaldo, Ronaldinho, Juninho and Kaka grew up playing indoor and outdoor concurrently until moving to the outdoor game to commence their professional careers. Australian soccer stars such as Mark Viduka, Marco Bresciano, Brett Emerton and Lucas Neill have also grown up in an environment devoted to small sided games and training methods. Each of these players identifies the Australian Institute of Sport as the place where they learned how to play properly and it is no coincidence that the AIS teaches a method/ style of play that is a hybrid of the South American short passing games.

Futsal's positive effects on the outdoor player were further endorsed by the brilliant Brazilian Juninho's impression that

> I think the best way to improve your skills is to play football on a smaller pitch. I didn't play 11-a-side football until I was 13 years old. In Brazil most kids play what we call Futebol de Salão, which is similar to five-a-side.

Perhaps for me, the notion which stood out from both reports was the NSW Premier Soccer Task Force Report's statement that futsal enhances creativity and problem solving in players.

Back in 2002, a little bit of creativity and problem-solving was certainly needed for me to get these Under 16 Blues up to speed so as not to embarrass themselves and me. I would have to move my tush because we had started our campaign very late.

I had very little time to create a team not without its own unique problems.

At all levels.

American Pulitzer Prize winning poet, Mary Oliver once scribbled that '… maybe just looking and listening is the real work'. As, to me, Oliver is the wisest human being in the world (you really should buy some of her books) I decided not to argue the toss and spent the next month listening to other coaches, inviting myself to their sessions and attempting to nut out what the hell rotation was and why it was useful in futsal.

My team was not short on character, only experience. Our democratically elected captain, Craig, was the only player who had experience at the national level of futsal and immediately asked me if we were going to play rotation. I told him we'd work on our basic skills first before we worried about things like rotation (which still sounded to me like a really dirty dance move). *As the team is new to the game,* I said to Craig, *I don't want to confuse them early on in the piece.* I thanked God, daily, that not one of the boys asked me if I was in fact new to the game as well and for which club I had played. As I've said on countless occasions, it's amazing how far you can get with a confident sounding voice and offering to 'get back' to people. Finally, my theatrical background provided me with something of practical use.

The six players I had in The Blues were a start, but I knew we'd need more than six. James had some natural flair and an in-built sneer which served as a defence mechanism against doubt – I could tell already that I would have to get his confidence up quickly; Luke was a cheeky monkey with a competitive attitude (who needed his skills to reach a similar level) and who seemed obsessed with using futsal as a mechanism for attracting members of the opposite sex, perhaps without realising we were an all-male team; Morto was a big-hearted player teetering on the edge of being outstanding or ordinary, depending on whether you chose and clicked the right switch; Ben was my quiet enforcer who rarely said boo but exploded into an uncompromising gear when on the court; and lastly Eric, who you literally had to put a bomb under to dazzle from his seemingly perpetual catatonic state, the promising thing being that when he was ignited he could unleash a rocket of a kick which I would not willingly put my bulk behind as a goalie – you would end up being taken with the ball into the back of the net. How to get these boys to sustain and believe in their gifts would be the rub.

Thankfully, I did not have to recruit too far and wide to make up the remaining numbers. Jann, bless her cotton socks, talked over a friend of Murray's who had not come in for the trials so I could have someone on the subs bench. Keith was a veritable brick shithouse and alongside Ben would prove a solid defensive wall. Eric, in a fit of energy, called his friend Daniel, who he assured me was 'pretty good', to come along for the ride. Hoping I wouldn't have a pair of slow fuses in the team, I was pleasantly surprised to find Daniel to be an aggressive, alert and determined player with a healthy striker's appetite. So that left the goalkeeper...

I remembered my Under 15 club side had had real trouble pushing anything past the Tuggeranong 'keeper. This outdoor side had won the competition and I can recall being impressed by the safe hands and reflexes of their goalie. I wasn't sure how I would approach recruiting him, but then I figured you can go far in life by just picking up a phone and asking people for things – trust me, it can work. So almost whimsically I called the Tuggers coach and asked if his impressive goalie would be interested in coming to Albury with my Blues-train. The coach said he would talk to Shane and when my phone rang minutes later I knew I had a full complement.

As I've found is common in all football sides I have coached over the years, my new team used more tubs of gel than a conference hall full of boy bands. So, at the very least, we would *look* very slick.

Off the field.

With a plethora of ACT teams booking indoor courts all over Canberra and the Nationals fast approaching, our early training experiences occurred pretty much wherever we could find a space: church halls, school halls, abandoned basketball courts and police boys clubs. To start, I adapted my outdoor drills to the indoor context and found a lot them worked – and at the very least got the boys to focus on the particular task at hand. However, distraction was never too far away with The Blues. You could be right in the middle of a complex explanation of an intricate passing drill and have Luke side up to you and enquire *So, H, what are the women like in Albury?*

Daniel and Eric were starting to look like a promising menace up front and even James was also persistently slotting them in (with a sneer). I praised him too enthusiastically and received a customary icy half-nod with a look which suggested I had insulted his mother. Craig kept muttering that he had never seen any of these drills before in his futsal experience – which would have been true – and I informed him that I was known for being 'unconventional' and that I would 'get back' to him. And even our sole, experienced, embittered, rotation-loving futsal veteran had to admit that attempting to get a shot past Ben or Keith, both of whom liked to sit at the back on the court in defence, was more frustrating than any of my drills. Both seemed to take any goal scored against them as a personal affront, while maintaining a steady, stoic and stony demeanour. And Morto, with his neatly-gelled hair and Cappa gear was definitely the team's lead singer – good-natured, gifted and erratic. I figured that if I could find the correct trigger to detonate his ability and passion, I would also have a dangerous, unpredictable player there. But what was the trigger for a kid like this?

I decided to try simple affirmation.

In fact, I decided that affirmation, enthusiasm and unrelenting support might go a long way with every one of the boys. I may have been wrong, but I felt at the time that they all seemed a little scarred in some way by their various and diverse sporting experiences. I desperately wanted to make this experience one which wouldn't add insult to past injury but also knew it would be difficult to untie those knots. To smooth the uncalm waters of their cranky souls. I asked them how they expected they would perform in Albury and the response confirmed my suspicions...

We're the rejects, H. Nobody expects us to win a game. The other team reckons we won't score a goal.

Do you expect to win a game? I asked.

Na.

Silence.

Is Tasmania in this competition? another queried.

Why?

Well, they don't have futsal there, I heard. So we'd have a chance against them.

Luke decided to change the mood and delivered a veritable monologue of hope and inspiration.

Listen up, fellers. We'll at least have a better time than the other teams, cos they're so serious and concentratin' on playin' and winnin' and shit so – get this – we'll score all the chicks! The Gold team are too busy doin' it with each other to give us any competition when it comes to the women...!

He looked at us all, nodding quickly and totally convinced that anything female in Albury was waiting to be serviced by the team.

I sighed. It was obvious I had just as much work to do on what was going on inside their heads than what to do with their feet when a futsal ball came their way.

Looking at the positives, the one thing I noticed in these makeshift training sessions was that The Blues were clinically proficient at penalties, especially Eric. That dastardly blight on the game was one area in which this lot, unlike a lot of my past teams, simply excelled. Any member of the team could step up and effortlessly *thwack* the ball past Shane, who, like me, was left wondering why they performed so eloquently with a still ball, yet when it was moving they would get incredibly flustered and send it, consistently, on its way to Queanbeyan. I made a mental note to watch their kicking actions and to make sure they kept their heads down and eyes on the ball on impact. Yet one thing was for sure: when Daniel, Eric and Keith struck the ball, it stayed struck. And when any of the remaining boys decided to move the ball in any given direction, it always went where intended. I made a second mental note to build upon their encouraging accuracy in placement, passing and finishing.

It goes to show, doesn't it? No matter how desperate things seem, there is always somewhere to start, something to work with. But even in my wildest dreams, I just couldn't imagine how or at what point our adept skills in penalty kicks would ever manifest themselves in the match situation to any great advantage.

I had organised a game against the Under 15 ACT Gold side, who were coached by a mystical guru named

Danny. It was during this scratch match that I became first acquainted with a defensive formation which would reappear like an old schoolmate throughout my life as a futsal coach...*The Box*. The Blues played better than I expected but had real trouble scoring against the 15s, whose defensive square-shape became ever harder to penetrate as the match wore on.

After the game, I asked Danny about...*The Box* and he grabbed his clipboard and marker. As he muttered the phrase *It's very simple*, and started feverishly sketching, I knew I was in trouble. I got the basic gist of what was going on, but realised that trying to explain this to my lads in the remaining training sessions would be nothing short of coaching suicide. I then casually asked him what he felt about rotation and once again, with an *It's very simple*, began to draw lots of squiggles, crosses, dots and arrows which left me with steam flying out of my ears.

So, you got all that? Danny asked, handing me a clipboard full of hieroglyphics.

It's very simple, I replied. *I guess teaching it to these guys in the time I have left would be pretty – er – daunting.*

We're leaving next week, right? Danny retorted.

I gave out an over-confident, Boy-have-I-got-my-work-cut-out-for-me laugh.

Good luck! said Danny like a grim executioner.

Despite his somewhat terse manner, I liked him. He didn't try to sound even a little bit confident that the team or its coach would have any success on that score. Everyone loves a realist.

As I walked away, I remember Morto asking me if we were going to play a training game against the Gold side. I replied that I didn't think it was worth it as 1) we had just lost to a team younger than us, 2) all that it would probably do is boost the Gold side's confidence and eradicate any that we might have had, and 3) something inside me was suggesting to use all the time left – which was essentially the following weekend – to get us as prepped as we possibly could get. He walked away but I stopped him.

The trick is to believe in yourself, Morto, up here (I tapped my head) *and in here as well* (I tapped my heart). *You guys talk like you're big men, but unless you really believe in the words you say, you've got as much chance of finding a nice girl in Albury – who likes you for what you really are – as the team has in actually winning a game.*

He nodded and left, checking that his gel had held throughout practice. And possibly thinking his coach was starting to sound dangerously like a school counsellor. I made a mental note to tell Morto that I felt he had it in him to be vice captain, but was distracted by Craig and subsequently forgot to pass on my vote of confidence.

So, we using rotation, H?

Na, I replied, *and sorry it's taken me so long to get back to you. Danny and I were just having an intense coachy sorta conversation about its virtues at this stage in an adolescent futsal player's development. After assessing the pros and cons, we've decided there are better strategies to utilise than rotation for you guys. From a player-captain's perspective, Craig, you'll just have to readjust your paradigm for Albury.*

He looked at me hard. *So I guess that's a no.*

I looked back at him blankly as he left. *Screw rotation,* I said under my breath, *whatever it is…*

Futsal ACT phoned to let me know that I needed my Level 1 qualifications before going to the Nationals. And naturally, they had arranged for me and a handful of other coaches to do the course…over the following weekend. I pleaded with them that I'd hardly had my boys together for any significant time at this point and was desperate to get a couple of sessions in on Saturday and Sunday to work a few rotations and stuff like that. Wisely, in retrospect, I was told there was nothing they could do about it as I had to be qualified to coach at the State level. The cheek of them!

Former Australian rep Simon Aitchison was taking the Level 1 course. I had coached his nephew, Daniel, to a Bill Turner Plate win a few years earlier in the outdoor game, so we had a connection of sorts there. Simon was excellent in catering for those of us new to the sport as well as those more experienced former players who were simply there to get a piece of paper. Keeping things simple and clear and wasting little time, Simon took us through the course briskly and effectively. In fact, he only totally lost me when we got into the more complex systems of rotation which some bright international teams apparently had used at the World Cup. I had a mental block to overcome here, but I took notes and spent my evenings (and the eventual bus trip to Albury) trying to make sense of it all.

When I explained my deficiencies and insecurities to Simon, I was grateful when he agreed to come out to the AIS prior to our departure for Albury to take The Blues for a session and share some of his expertise. As I had coached his nephew, I figured we were great mates from way back and introduced him as if we had played alongside each other in a past World Cup campaign. It was all very impressive, really.

Once again, a real impression was made by The Blues, who were now regularly and pleasantly surprising me. Perhaps less prone to being know-alls as some Gold teams can be, The Blues soaked up Simon's expertise, suggestions and challenges like sponges. As he did with me during the course, he kept it simple and focused on positive outcomes and was immensely patient when things weren't clear or were slow in happening. Tellingly, during this session, no mention of the word 'winning' ever occurred. (And Luke did not mention 'hot chicks'. Not even once in passing.) The lads were so focused on a process that was so clearly developing them as players that peripheral concerns seemed irrelevant if not counterproductive to the good work they were doing.

And when some of the Aitchison drills mimicked what I had been doing with the boys in previous sessions, even their wobbly coach could leave the AIS after that last training with a little more confidence and satisfaction than when he entered.

We stepped off the bus in Albury, with Luke the first off. He looked to his left and right five or six times and assumed that the parade of nubile, nymphette-cheerleaders from southern New South Wales wearing wet '16 Blues' T-shirts must have got the date and place wrong.

As we were unpacking our gear from the bus, it was then I noticed how much the other Under 16 team were keeping to themselves. They sat together, unpacked together, dressed the same and even appeared to move like a clique of bitchy girls in the high school cafeteria. The only exception to the rule tended to be when they saw the need to put down any members of The Blues (or younger teams) usually out of earshot or vision of Chris D'Silva or myself. I was happy to see Murray distancing himself from this sort of negative behaviour and in many ways thought, given a choice, he might have been happier in the less intense atmosphere I had to offer.

My lads were obviously nervous and manifesting this anxiety through violence towards inanimate objects. I decided to take The Blues for a walk of the city streets after the customary dinner / food-fight but, as you already know, that just produced more of the same sort of mindless activity. It would seem that most of my team approached a sporting event as if it were a vicious dogfight or definitive test of their masculinity.

170

Or lack of it. Albury garbage bins beware.

I now literally had hours to convince them that it wasn't about these things at all. But my major problem was that I still wasn't totally believing my own rhetoric and, like my confusion with rotation and box defence, found it hard to clearly define in my head just exactly what it was all about. So when we went for that fatal walk along the streets of the soul, it seemed the only one of us having a placid yet unsettling existential moment was me.

That was until Morto picked up that branch and expressed, without eloquence or subtlety, our collective self-doubts.

The round-matches were diabolical. I could only take solace in the fact that all eight teams participating were certain to make the quarter-finals. We finished dead last, which meant we would play the first-placed side: ACT Gold. Funny how these things happen.

We got thumped by teams from New South Wales, Victoria and Queensland and, in the end, keeping the scores down to single digits became our main imperative. To add insult to injury, in the final round match Keith took a nasty knock to his leg, which effectively ended the tournament for one of our strongest defenders. While there had been passages of play which highlighted our individual strengths, even a complete stranger could tell this shadow side from the ACT were not reaching anywhere near their full potential. The Blues obviously gelled their hair a lot better than they gelled in playing as a team.

I was starting to feel that despite my unwritten and unwavering concern and care for these rogues, I could not find that catalyst to make them fire as a unit, convert their gradually increasing skill and tactical development to the game context, or channel some of their more directionless and aggressive adolescent energy productively onto the court. If I could harness whatever it was that made Morto pick up that stick and inexplicably whack a garbage bin, I'd have enough fuel to create a far happier, integrated, mentally and physically tougher and possibly soulful little team. I knew that the answer lay in being positive and fighting this undertow of wanton crankiness. As the Dalai Lama says in *The Art of Living*,

> With a pessimistic attitude, you cannot accomplish even something you could easily achieve. Whereas even if something is difficult to achieve, if you have an unshakeable determination there is eventually the possibility of achievement.

As I had become a living symbol of unwavering and gritty faith to these boys – which they had rarely experienced before (outside of their mums) – it was crucial that I stood tall when whacked or scraped by life's branches. If I cracked under the pressure, it would simply confirm their own pessimistic rage against the machine and contempt for its fickle, self-serving adults and repressive institutions. It would attest that the world was a miserable place where only the bastards get to enjoy the spoils. And the girls.

So I persisted. But instead of losing myself in manuals, books and copious notes, I took Mary Oliver's advice to 'Squander the day and save the soul'. In the spaces between fixtures, I put my feet up and watched older teams from all states playing the game, particularly noting those which effectively 'rotated'. I repeated in my head Mary O's maxim that the real work was to look and to listen. Then, as stubborn as ever, I called the boys for meetings on the lawns outside the playing centre where I decided to try to teach the team, once and for all, the concept of rotation and hence increase my own understanding as I taught it. Better late than never.

The Under 15s were playing on another court and I sat myself on a nearby bench and watched greedily as my guru's side executed…*The Box* with consummate poise and skill. They even threw in a few snazzy rotations and really looked the money. So I observed. Listened. Recorded. Reflected. I can remember wondering if I would ever exert such a fantastic influence on one of my sides; provide them with something practical and nifty and clever which they could then explore and utilise to full effect in front of an appreciative audience of parental admirers. An important thing I also noticed was that while Danny's team were not always winning, the parents didn't give a flying pig. Why would they? The team was playing creative, thoughtful and intricate futsal. Except to a total idiot, it was clear that they had evolved into a team which would eventually win as a result of their development as players, over and above the immediate need for a national title. It was great to see a young side given a structure from which they could then build with increased confidence and creativity. As a theatre director, I had always felt assured that I could give that much to my actors, a secure base upon which to explore and develop and create a characterisation that is both theirs and mine.

It may not always provide immediate, gratifying dividends such as a national title or a theatre award at glitzy ceremonies, but I have no doubt that, in time, this approach does provide so very much more.

I'd found some space to have some quiet time in the late afternoon the day before the quarter-finals and was reading Tibor Fischer's wonderful novel *Under the Frog*, about the lives of two basketballers in Hungary plying their trade in the years leading up to the uprising of 1956. I was moved by a passage in which Fischer describes one of the many joys of coaching:

> Gyuri had learned from his own coaching...that the greatest part of the pleasure was seeing the invisible strings pulled, relishing the remote control, like being a theatre director or general. You wanted to recognise your handiwork.

Fischer's words echoed my thoughts of the previous day and left me wondering, once again, if I would ever recognise any of my own handiwork in these scallywags. As it was late and nearing sundown, I could feel the blues creeping in and was beginning to wish I had stayed at home – that I had never impulsively said 'yes' to Jann a month or so ago – when Luke cleared his throat at the doorway. His big desperate, hopeful, guppy eyes pre-empted a request which I knew would push any coach's acceptable boundaries.

H?

Yes, Luke.

Would you get us another video?

Aren't you enjoying The Spy Who Shagged Me?

That's not quite the sort of video we were after…

Absolutely not, Luke. Go away. I'm reading.

What about some magazines?

Luke, I am your coach. Not your big brother. Or supplier. I will not do anything illegal for you, like buying cigarettes or booze or dirty picture books.

There's not as many chicks in Albury as we hoped.

Were you really expecting them to be lining the streets in G-strings? Take a reality check. Sometimes things aren't quite what you expect in life.

He nodded five or six times.

I persisted. *Has this trip been what you expected?*

Yeah. We've been getting whipped. But we're getting better. Having fun. I knew we'd have fun.

Are you having fun out on the court?

We will tomorrow when we smash those gay homosexuals in the Gold team.

I was thinking about explaining the concept of tautology to Luke but decided against it. He winked at me and, like a typical, cheeky adolescent, scarpered as the conversation veered towards seriousness. But just before he was out of earshot I yelled out to him to inform Morto that he'd be playing in the back two tomorrow – in place of Keith. He better not let me down.

I heard a *Will do, H!* from down the corridor and found myself alone with my book once more. Strangely, Luke had left me feeling more positive than I had felt only moments earlier. The boys were obviously *looking forward* to tomorrow, had in no way discounted a chance at giving the Gold team a run for their money and, perhaps most importantly, were still having fun. I had forgotten about that key element of enjoyment. So the trip had not been a failure on quite a few counts. For all my talk, maybe the only person lacking any belief in the chance of a boil-over tomorrow was me. I found myself tapping myself on the head. And over the heart. Sheesh. I may well have been working the invisible strings, but, like an actor, had to start to believe more fully in what I was doing in order to allow the handiwork of all those rehearsals to produce something special on the big stage. Only then can you be truly satisfied in what you are doing.

Right at the point that I was insanely tapping various

parts of my body, I was disturbed by the Gold team. They were arriving home from dinner, all wearing flashy shirts, their hair stylishly gelled and a whole dust cloud of attitude puffing in their wake like car exhaust. I wanted to yell out *Hi* to Murray and wish him all the best for tomorrow but decided that this wouldn't be the best for him or myself. The Gold team didn't need any luck after all.

Next, by way of contrast, my boys came skidding past my hotel door daggily screaming and shouting at the tops of their lungs. They were playing tag and throwing ice cubes at each other (which they had stolen from the hotel kitchen). In fact, they clearly were behaving worse than the Under 11s after a couple of raspberry spiders. I sighed again. Evidently, playing tag with ice cubes was better entertainment than watching Mike Meyers and a slightly healthier alternative to dubious pictorial pleasure. With my totally ineffective voice of mock-annoyance, I told them to settle down and go to bed as it was getting late.

Besides, I didn't want them to wake the Under 11s.

So there we were in the quarter-finals. Friendless and

girlfriendless, gormless and pornless, and very much winless. But after watching and hearing the Gold team continue to denigrate and dismiss my Blues Brothers throughout the previous evening and again over breakfast cereal, like my boys, just at the point where I was going to give in to the seemingly depressing inevitability of it all, I felt a renewed vigour and motivation not to go down without a fight. I was singing Queen's 'We Are the Champions' in my room while packing my kit for the day, when I noticed Luke at the door.

What you singing that for? In case you hadn't realised, we haven't won a game yet. And according to the Gold team, we aren't going to today either.

All I could do was respond in song:

And bad mistakes
I've made a few
I've had my share of sand kicked in my face
But I've come through

I looked back at my team's Casanova wondering if I had inspired him.

H, the guy that wrote that song's a huge fag. I wouldn't sing it around other people if I was you.

I apologised and promised to bring my Marilyn Manson tapes on the next tour.

At the stadium, instead of an intricate, complex and showy warm-up, I pulled the boys over for a conversation.

Do you think we can win this?

A lot of silence and a distant *Maybe* was all I got.

Fellers, we've been working as long and as hard as the Gold team to make a fist of things here at these Nationals. Have you guys heard some of the things they have been saying about you...?

I pulled out my notebook and began to read a list of things which they had said (and some of which they hadn't) insinuating that my Blues had sex with everything from their immediate family to farm animals, followed closely by a list of unsavoury and unnatural acts which served as a metaphor for what the Gold team were apparently going to do to my helpless team. Gotta love late adolescence. The only way of describing, relating or even intimidating them into action seems to be through gratuitous reference to the long sought-after bonk.

Did they say all that? asked Luke incredulously.

I nodded, noticing that even my team's quieter members had that look of mass murder in their eyes indicating that finally a little more than just the game was at stake. I had offended their attention. But I pulled back on the reins.

You know, boys, if I've learned anything in my fifteen years of coaching, the trick is not to go out there with venom. The trick is to go out there and play your game. Enjoy playing it. Enjoy each other. Venom has no place. Anger hasn't either. Do not go out there stirred up and angry and try to wipe them off the court, because then you start playing someone else's game and bring other unwanted, complicated things into what should be a simple forty minutes. Remember, when a bee uses its stinger, it dies. So let's not kill a part of ourselves by using our stingers. Let's use the stuff we all do so well: accurate passes, strong shots on goal and, if applicable, pinpoint penalty-taking.

But how do we beat them, H? asked Morto.

By not worrying about beating them. In not responding to them like you did at the hotel, at breakfast and on the bus on the way here. Don't get provoked to use your stinger, as you may need it in more desperate situations.

They provoked us with what they said, H.

181

Then smile and agree with them.

They said some pretty nasty things about what we do to each other at night, H…

And that's because they're not getting any either.

Some low neanderthalic chuckles.

I continued, *Focus on the game. Because, if you ignore their taunts, you will unsettle them more. Because they are just as insecure as you are — they just have a few more ball skills when they play a futsal game. So if you can get the upper hand early — you may rattle them a little. Then if they start getting physical, you do NOT retaliate. You keep playing the game instead of proving you can be as pathetic as they are. Accumulate the fouls and then maybe you'll find you'll even have a chance of winning the game.*

There was a brief moment of silence. My God, they were not only looking at me, they were listening. And considering.

And what about rotation? asked Craig.

Do you all know how to use it now?

They all nodded, confidently. Those sessions on the lawns had been quality time. I sensed it was down to me now. At this moment in the STAS Continuum, I felt rotations and box-defences were intricacies best left for another dimension. What was needed here were fundamentals, the basics, done well. After all, this was not about me mixing it as a coach with the Dannys and Simons and Chrises of this world.

Bugger rotation, I replied. *Play* your *game. Not someone else's.*

We took the lead early. Eric and Daniel were in scintillating form. We only had a few chances, essentially due to the Gold side being lazy. We slotted each and every one. I knew things were looking up when Luke latched onto a loose ball and slotted it home. I could see him about to say something to their (previously) outspoken goalie who had some nasty things to say about Luke's sexual prowess earlier in the week, but was proud to see the boy stop himself, turn round and run back into position for the restart. That was a massive moment in his growth, totally unseen by the world.

Stepping into Keith's shoes would be no mean feat, but Morto did it with gusto. Partnering Ben at the back, the newly formed dynamic duo consistently stopped some arrogant attacking forays by the Gold side straight through the guts, an attack which was focusing more on busting through the defence than working a way around it. They scored a few goals using brawn, but not enough to keep up with our goals, usually scored on the counterattack or by some slick passing moves which were finally paying off.

When opposition goals went in, I could see Shane taking the blame for each of them somewhere deep inside. I called out his name and gave him a 'there-there' signal with my hands, then pointed a finger to my head and my heart. I think he got the message.

By half-time, we had scored more goals than we had managed in the entire series of pool matches. We were ahead 4–3 and spectating vultures, sensing a boil-over, hovered in droves from far and wide to cheer the underdogs over the line and maybe get to peck at a potential champion's carcass. This had a savage effect on the Gold side, who were used to receiving attention as winners not as potential losers. In the second half, with the bigger crowd in attendance, the Golden guys tried even harder to use brute force to score and, before they knew it, had accumulated four fouls. (Once again, for the uninitiated, after five fouls you get a free penalty kick – one on one with the 'keeper – every time a foul is committed.) I looked up and saw that Luke, boosted by his goal, was starting to enjoy himself immensely and his cheeky grin would have been enough to turn a nun rabid. James was on the bench at this point and his sneer was – yes, quite possibly – straightening into a smile. The Gold side kept trying to crunch Luke and, in trying to halt Daniel and Eric's unrelenting march forward, starting to commit even more unnecessary fouls.

I turned to look at Chris D'Silva who was sitting on the other bench, his head slumped into his hands in disgust and disfavour. It was then I truly believed we had a chance here. The Gold team was not playing their usual fluid game and were totally overcome and possibly distracted by their own hype. This was, after all, supposed to be a cruisy win and when the script changed, like many teams too used to winning, they were very slow to adapt. It is a good argument for spontaneity and unpredictability when playing flashy, champion sides.

As Luke was sent flying into the next court, he landed with a thud and looked up with those guppy eyes which would have easily secured him a role as one of the cute little sisters in *Little House on the Prairie*. The ref nearly blasted the whistle out of his mouth, pointed at the penalty spot and gave us the first of a sequence of penalty kicks. Eric stepped up and, milliseconds after the ref blew the whistle, the ball was already in the back of the net before anyone even realised he had lined himself up. Eric wasn't prone to farting around. Now two goals in arrears, the Gold team came perilously close to falling apart. Every time they reduced the deficit to one goal, they would give away a silly foul and we'd get another penalty kick. With a marksman's precision, Eric would then clinically dispatch the ball into the back of the net before the goalie could even ponder saying something disparaging about his mum. I remember thinking how much I loved penalties and how great they were for the game. With minutes left, we were still ahead by two goals when a nasty, late tackle saw Morto sprawled on the floor in agony grabbing his ankle.

The ref blew the whistle to hold up the game but strangely did not give us a penalty kick this time. As I dragged Morto away from the game, I feared this break in momentum might be just what the Gold team needed to recompose itself. I was unfortunately correct. I made the sub but, just seconds after Craig ran on to the field, the Gold side instantly pulled a goal back. I wanted to be back with the boys on the bench, up near the sideline talking them through all this but ,with no one around to help me treat the injured player, I became trapped with Morto, who was in agony at the opposite side of the court.

The Gold side levelled with about a minute to go, and the dam had broken. Sniffing an improbable victory from the jaws of defeat and finally using their skills instead of muscle, the Gold side put through the winning goal and then another to be certain with seconds left in the match.

Morto's face was as twisted as his ankle and for a second that's how my soul felt too. I said to him, *We won that game, Morto. In here and in here.*

Dear reader, you know where I was pointing.

As I was starting to pick up the shattered remains of my team, Danny sauntered over and said with his characteristic sensitivity, *Well, you guys butchered that one good and proper, didn't yous!*

The Victorian and New South Wales coaches came over and gave me congratulations for taking it to the ACT Gold side. They gave me thanks for exposing to them weaknesses which they hadn't seen in the Gold side previously. They mustn't have been the brightest of blokes, as ACT Gold then went on to effortlessly win the title and put a smile back on Chris D'Silva's face. I remember the Queensland coach quizzing me about what had created the drastic transformation in my side from easy-beats in the preliminary games to potential giant-killers in the quarterfinal. I said something banal about things needing to matter in order to motivate us but it wasn't what I meant or even wanted to say.

I meant to say that the boys had got better because they had developed *from* their losses rather than being defeated by them. They took what they could use from defeat and then simply let defeat go. The team's strength, which I recognised far too late was unlike that of other teams, was that they were never intrinsically success-orientated. Something had killed that in them well before they got to me. So they came on this tour to enjoy themselves and their indoor soccer, impervious to the doubt, pressure, heaviness and goo which constantly having to prove yourself can bring. As a result, they could intuitively embrace a notion very close to *kaizen* more easily than most; they could all develop at a greater rate than their more talented peers because, purely and simply, as people *and* players, winning was never really an issue to them. Not even a remote issue.

I knew that, even though we had lost, this loss would be as sweet if not sweeter than cruising through a bunch of pool games and effortlessly taking out the title. We felt like champions, that's for sure. And on paper, we hadn't won a thing.

Unfortunately, the boys did all they could to try my patience further. It is perhaps best not to mention my having to drag them out of a nightclub well after curfew that night. Then lecturing them about winning so much respect in the public arena and then doing their damnedest to lose it a few short hours later. And then herding them into a Hungry Jack's when on the return trip (I made them walk silently in single file) the lot of us nearly got our heads smacked in by hovering Albury hoons in panel vans out looking for a fight. Luke was about to hurl some thoughtless abuse at the locals when I assured him, quietly, that if the hoons didn't knock him out I certainly would if he didn't shut his big fat mouth.

But nothing, really, could taint their achievements only hours earlier. The tables and record books will always state that we won absolutely nothing. But a lot of significant inroads were made by The Blues and some scars even seemed to be healing.

That loopy American general, George S. Patton, once said, 'I don't measure a man's success by how high he climbs but how high he bounces when he hits the bottom.' Well, let me tell you about the bouncers. Eric and Daniel both made it into the Gold side after their outstanding performance at the Nationals, and won the ensuing National Championships. (From last to first place in six months! That's not bad.) An unrecognisably hairy Ben appeared in a winning Erindale team at the Schools' titles last year in Brisbane, playing as doggedly as ever. And most of the team received invites to tour internationally with Queensland Futsal's 'Australian' team tours.

But perhaps the major thing about this whole journey was that it was obvious from all of their faces, particularly at half-time in that quarter-final, that the boys had refound the capacity to *surprise* themselves. (Adolescents try so very hard to look, live and act like nothing surprises them any more.) And that, to me, is one of the more lasting memories I will ever take from sport. How, through this ridiculous activity we do with balls and nets and whistles and flags, there lies the capacity for a human being to realise and release a more creative, determined, positive, new and permanent aspect of themselves which they may not have realised existed.

I remember talking to Morto on the phone when he informed me he had been chosen for an Australian tour as a result of his performance in the quarter-final match. I congratulated him and asked him if he had smashed any unsuspecting bin lids lately. He played dumb, asking me again what I thought about the team's amazing transformation across the Albury series. I sang in response.

It's been no bed of roses
No pleasure cruise -

Morto butted in. *Please don't sing, H.*

I recognised long ago that singing in public really upsets teenagers. So I stopped and said instead, *You're a champ, Morto.*

Thanks, H. So are you. Will you coach us again?

I knew it would never happen but I said, *If you stay together. There's only so much you can achieve at one competition. You need to give time for things – for a team – to grow...*

Seeya next year then, H.

I didn't. Life proved too distracting for all of us. Or maybe – just maybe – those cheerleaders finally showed up.

George S. Patton, that outspoken general I've already quoted once in this chapter, apparently said (shortly before his death in a car accident), 'Boys, in my book, coming second is just as bad as coming last.' It was a shame he wasn't around for this little jaunt with The Blues. We came nowhere near second – dead set last, in fact, but as far as we all were concerned, we had got more out of our time in Albury than most of the teams above us. And here we still were, months later, feeling like champions. Perhaps more so than the eventual winners.

It was all so easy to see now that The Blues had left me. You can be champions without winning a single game. It's a hard point to make to some people.

But I'll keep on fighting till the end...

13: Tails

The Ladies' Men

I'm shittin' me balls.

Charles Turnbull

We can score some cheap points here...

Charles Turnbull

I read in an *Inside Sport* article that, when all is said and done with his international career, Australian goalkeeper and captain Mark Schwarzer felt that he could find happiness and love in being coach of the Bondi United Under 12s. And if someone as cool, collected, successful and nice as Mark Schwarzer can look an interviewer in the eye and say things like that, I figure there is still some hope for sporting humanity. But I suspect, in my heart of hearts, that even someone as accomplished as Schwarzer would come to find that simply attending a sporting event these days is no easy task.

Yet I imagine that, from his Premier League experiences, Schwarzer would be used to working around those who place an uncomfortable and insatiable value on winning and tax you with massive demerit points on losing. When you are unsuccessful, coaching can make you feel like a busted drunken driver… You knew you shouldn't have got behind the steering wheel and, when you did, you not only publicly embarrassed yourself but could have caused long-lasting, irreparable, if not lethal, damage to others.

And then look at the *successful* coaches in Junior Sport. Let's face it: they're essentially sober, humourless bunnies who remind me of those body snatchers from bad Hollywood fifties sci-fi who often choose to sit, uncomfortably, in the skin of some balding or grey-haired fat guy with a nervous disorder (such as savage twitching). They then spend a lot of their earthly time inflicting their dull, heartless and insidious plans for world domination upon their unsuspecting charges, who mistakenly think they are human. They devise fun-free sequences of preparatory drills and mountain sprints akin to a bad day with the drill sergeant from *Starship Troopers*. OK, maybe I am going a little too far here, but it seems increasingly rare these days that coaches take their charges to the top of the dungheap with rational, sensitive, new-age, amiable and nice coaching technique.

This raises the question, why exactly is an unhealthy proportion of the grumpy, the arrogant and/or the distinctly if not clinically aggressive always so damned successful at sport? In that same Schwarzer article, I remember reading Paul Barron's assessment of the Socceroo goalkeeper:

> Mark Schwarzer's only weakness is possibly also his greatest strength... He is too nice a guy – if you can call that a failing. He could improve his game by being a bit more horrible to people!

This, in turn, raises another disturbing question: is it in fact possible to be immensely successful as a coach or participant in sport without being horrible, arrogant, grumpy and psychotically intense? And, if the answer is *No*, we should ask again, what constructive use can sport possibly be to our children? I remember hearing American actor James Caan remark in an interview that 'the most talented people I've worked with are the nicest'. So surely, just surely, there must be a chance for the 'nice' to achieve some successful outcomes in sport beyond the lucky Bondi United Under 12 team. At least once in a while.

All I can say is thank God for Hollywood.

At the very least, in every celluloid depiction of a sporting journey I've ever seen, nice guys don't always finish last. If it weren't for *The Bad News Bears*, *Rocky I, II, III, IV, V, VI, VII, VIII* and *IX – The Nursing Home Challenge*, the entire Star Wars series, *The Mighty Ducks*

I, II and *III, Mystery Alaska, Remember the Titans* and even *Dodgeball,* I'd possibly never have believed that the underdogs or any motley collection of essentially 'nice' folk would even have a snowflake's hope in hell of ever making it to the top. Or thereabouts.

So towards the end of 2003, convinced that the only victories I would ever achieve in coaching were through the triumph of the soul, and armed with a developing premonition of *kaizen,* I decided, just for once, to attempt coaching as a 'nice' guy to see what would happen. I was prepared for a good dose of spiritual happiness despite a load of dirty, dusty disappointment with a light sprinkling of disillusionment.

The challenge wasn't quite what I expected.

Schwarzer got the age group correct. But it was from Canberra, not Bondi, where the miraculous team emerged from.

Enter The Ladies' Men...

Is there anything harder to analyse, predict or categorise than a twelve-year-old boy? Despite the fact that I used to hang out with them twenty-six years ago, I hadn't had all that much experience with any of their kind of late or any useful, practical knowledge and insight into what actually makes them tick. In fact, if the truth be known, despite my many years of teaching experience, their inner and outing workings flummox me as much as farm machinery.

In 2003, Radford decided to send some teams to the National Schools Futsal Championships in Brisbane. The decision proved popular, as we had five teams formed of all shapes, sizes and genders before the permission slips had so much as been sent out. For reasons I still cannot fathom – except my obvious attraction to chaos and uncertainty – I suggested to the other coaches that we all take age groups outside our usual parameters of experience. With many members of my present Under 17 outdoor side having to participate in the Under 19 competition (the age groupings jumped from Under 16s to 19s), I had no intention or desire to revisit the bin-bending, late adolescent challenges of the Albury experience. So I volunteered to take the Under 12 Boys thinking I'd be cradling a red wine and happily falling off to sleep, dribbling in a motel chair before 8 p.m. while the other coaches would be frantically running around trying to keep their charges in their respective rooms and out of seedy bars.

In any case, my good friend, Jann, whose father Jack Lennard (an Olyroo from the 1956 Olympics) had recently passed away, was keen to coach Murray, in what looked liked one final fling at a national schools' title. This had been eluding her in past attempts and I knew she had been hoping to win in memory of her dear father. Although sometimes this sort of motivation can pressure sport into assuming a more complex weighting than it needs to, I could personally empathise with Jann's sentiments. Any time something pleasant or profound occurs along the STAS Continuum, I always feel the presence of my father, leaning against some post or tree slightly away from the hullabaloo, gently puffing away on a cigarette and enjoying things from a safe, serene distance.

The school, at this stage, had an entry point at Year 7, so finding eligible players was not as easy as it seemed. For starters, I had to go the Administration Block and (after three coffees, twenty-seven Monte Carlos and fifteen minutes of maternal realignment) left with a pristine print-out of all those ankle-biters who would still only be twelve years of age at the end of 2003. To my despair, the list was shorter than a hobbit's lectern. It had fewer than a dozen names on it.

I obviously had to do something about this, so I threw caution to the wind and ventured down to the ovals at lunchtime to where the Year 7 boys were playing a passionate game of something slightly resembling soccer – with a tinge of gaelic football, fox hunting and dwarf-throwing. As an airborne munchkin chased by a hundred rabid ewoks flew (quite literally horizontally) past my line of vision, I grabbed at a few lively lads who I knew played soccer as they *pinged* past me. I asked them if they could conjure an indoor team of seven out of the remaining names on my short shortlist. After much straining, furrowing, frowning and head-scratching (as thinking is in fact a hard thing for a Year 7 boy to do at lunchtime), they asked me why exactly I wanted to 'con-jar' an indoor side.

When I mentioned a possible trip to Brisbane I could instantly see the bikinis in their eyes. God love 'em. And as I am largely considered cool by Year 7's standards because a) they are easy to fool, b) we share the same intellectual capacity, c) their aesthetic tastes are reasonably similar to mine – I like Kiss, they like Britney, both wear make-up – and d) we both pathologically enjoy poking fun at ludicrous authority figures, the thought of going interstate with H would have all the attraction of a seven-day fun-park jaunt with free entry, unlimited rides and all-you-can-eat fairy floss. I did warn them it was winter so they might not see as many bikinis as they initially thought.

We could score some cheap points! Charlie informed me. (Little kids, like people from India, always talk with exclamation marks.)

And I suspected Charlie wasn't just talking about scoring in the sports arena either. Any idea I had that I would be taking an innocent bunch of pre-pubescent choirboys to Queensland was quickly dispelled as we tried to work out a name for our potential combo. We were definitely more creative at naming than Futsal ACT.

How about 'The Ladies' Men'? suggested Tuckers, who up until that point I thought was the most modest, unassuming, pensive, angelic and most-likely-to-do-missionary-work-in-Calcutta of the team.

There followed excited if not downright filthy chortles as the boys scurried off to work out the best way in which to garner inexpensive pointage while away from their mothers on tour. Little boys have a propensity to disappear in a *ping* when they have their minds set on something – regardless of the restrictions of commonsense, budget or danger – or whenever someone mentions the cleaning-up of anything. So by the time permission slips and itineraries had even been drafted, I am reasonably sure the boys already had gallons of hair gel, repulsive adolescent deodorant brands, truly awful Lowes shirts and a futsal ball, all thrown into their smelly kitbags still rank from winter rain. At the very least, I was relieved that they thought to pack something related to sport – like a ball – as indoor soccer seemed to be a distant fourth on their list of tour perks behind 1) Chicks, 2) Their Hair and 3) *Hangin' Out Wif Da H-man!* (that's me) in Brissie.

Luckily the team had selected itself – any entity under twelve years old who was bothered enough to get their parents to fill in a permission form made it into The Ladies' Men. Experience in lunchtime soccer, gaelic footy, fox-hunting or dwarf-throwing seemed requisite enough to me. So, for a second major futsal adventure, I didn't have to worry about the pains of trials, just the painful trials of training.

I had recently been reading Stan Alves's somewhat ominously titled autobiography *Sacked Coach* for inspiration, and was taken by a passage about champions and self-motivation:

> Others can guide and encourage and that's really important. But if you rely on them for your motivation it's like trying to walk through life shackled to a ball and chain. Only you can do it. That means putting yourself firmly behind the wheel and taking personal control of everything that happens in your life.

As suggested, I was determined to remain nice and nifty and New Age in my approach with these lads and,

201

inspired by the fired Alves – who I figured had never been tainted by success of any kind – asked the boys what drills they'd like to do; what they thought was important to practise and develop; what their long-term goals might be (Charlie: *Scoring cheap points, H – I told you that already!*); what their dreams might be (Charlie, again: *Scoring cheap points with Britney Spears!*); and, like a true hippy endowed with not even a cell of reality or common sense, I let them determine a large proportion of their preparatory sessions. I had put them firmly behind the wheel. As Shakespeare wrote in *Cymbeline*, 'Fortune brings in some boats that are not steered.' And who the hell could argue with The Bard?

I knew instinctively we'd do a lot of shooting drills, as that's all boys – be they little or big – really want to do in their heart of footballing hearts. Should we look at other important aspects of futsal like ball skills, team formation and fitness? *Hell, no!* said one. *Why?* said another. *They're boring!* added a third. In fact, the lot of them looked at me as if I had offered them a tuna casserole.

We trained on Friday afternoons, after school, which again was their choice. And can I say categorically, here and now, that any coach looking at this timeslot as a potential training time should, while still on the phone, book an appointment with their shrink, as they'll be most definitely gnawing off their own arms by the end of the session. When school concludes on Friday at 3.30 p.m., so does any hope of discipline, inspiration or motivation until some indeterminable point midway through the following Saturday. Thankfully, it was at these unproductive, sometime cantankerous Friday arvo sessions that I discovered that this unique and likeable bunch of boys had an Achilles heel – they all got sleepy at 6.00 p.m. and wherever they were, whatever the context, they would go to sleep there and then: on the dunny, under the shower, flying down a superslide, halfway through eating a pizza and, somewhat unfortunately, on the playing field.

I remember at one of the trials wondering where the slightly-confused-yet-nonetheless-puppy-eyed goalkeeper Wozza had disappeared to (that is, a puppy which looks as if it has been whacked over the head with a large plank) as I noticed the boys practising their finishing into an empty goal.

He's over there! Aidan informed me in his matter-of-fact, unflappable, nothing-really-surprises-me manner of speaking. (It was for these qualities I had made Aidan the captain. Besides being three times the size of the nearest member of TLM, I figured he was the only member of the team who could concentrate long enough to decide which side of the coin to choose at kick-off. In fact, I suspect he was the only one who knew the options. I had a secret hope that Aidan had in fact had his *ping* gland removed at birth and correctly felt that making a decision such as *Heads or Tails?* would not cause too much steam to fly out of his ears. This was certainly the case on the field, where Aidan was always ice-cool in his dealing with the many sporting choices and possibilities presented to a young player. But without being too rude, the reality was, off the field, I would become increasingly surprised if Aidan didn't turn up to school in his pyjamas. On a Saturday. Aidan was the sort of kid who, when he woke up in the morning, needed to be told fairly quickly which suburb if not solar system he lived in before being guided gently down the hall.)

Wozza, meanwhile, was asleep on a bench. He'd just had enough and, mid-drill, unequivocally decided to cease training – and consciousness for the day – and go to sleep right there and then on a hard plank of wood. I recalled Michael Parkinson's analysis of goalkeepers in *On Football*, where he stated that 'they are as much a mystery in the general order of things as the function of the human appendix.'

I've got to go to Rep training! Al announced next, readjusting some recalcitrant gel.

Behind him, Sundo was just standing still trying hard to remember where he actually was and why.

Rhys was kicking an imaginary flaming soccer ball in an intense scenario involving a team full of ninjas on skateboards.

Charlie was no doubt thinking about Britney Spears's hooters.

And angelic Tuckers was in the process of politely articulating some serious if not scientific doubts that we'd ever be ready for competitive fixtures in Brisbane.

I was not going to lose my temper.

No!

I had promised myself this at the start of the Be-Mark-Schwarzer-Nice Campaign Trail. *Remember, George, I told myself, the New Age of Coaching has begun.* Breathe in. Breathe out. Wax on. Wax off. Sally, Rhys's mum and TLM's manager, as well as the coach's personal spiritual trainer, could sense that I was 'in a potentially bad space' and went out and bought me a cappuccino and a cheesecake.

I'm not sure how this all looked to neutral observers.

So I just left Wozza, our team's mystifying appendix, snoring on the bench and covered him with my crumb-filled Manchester United jacket. Then, wiping the seeds of passionfruit icing from the corners of my mouth and sounding like a Telstra operator on acid, I wished Al all the best for his training; gave Sundo some geographical landmarks in order to determine his longitude and latitude; provided Rhys with a real ball and a set of make-believe nunchucks; refocused Charlie on scoring in the soccer context; and reassured Tuckers that, regardless of what happened, we were going to have an unforgettable experience together.

I was right on that score.

We played some training games against the slightly older Under 13s boys' team and the Under 14 girls' side which I tactfully scheduled well before sundown. I'm sure one of the scorelines was closer than the other but, regardless, the matches gave me a chance to work out where to play all The Ladies' Men who, no doubt, scored some cheap points during and after the latter fixture.

I had started Sundo in goal and despite the fact he only had to face in one direction he didn't seem too orientated or comfy there. Wozza volunteered to go in

– Just for training, OK! – but ended up being so acrobatic, if not AFL in his 'keeping style that I knew from that day I would con-jar a cunning way of leaving him in there.

Tuckers, in his usual mix of altruism and aristocracy, informed me, *I will play wherever you deem appropriate, Mr Huitker, or wherever I might be most effective for the team!*

As I was short on defenders, I earmarked him for the back line and also figured he could work as a compass for Sundo as well as a somewhat terse yet astute analyst and interpreter of strategy for the team.

Not that I think it matters, Mr Huitker, Tuckers bumbled on, *as on present form we are likely to be in for a good old-fashioned shagging in Brisbane!* I thanked him for his blunt evaluation and pointed out that if that were the case we'd all at least score a great big bundle of cheap points.

The remaining four Ladies' Men – Aidan, Al, Charlie and Rhys – all had attacking flair (and, like most forwards, an addiction to hair gel) – and it became glaringly apparent in training sessions and games that perhaps this was all we could effectively do – attack, attack, attack. I correctly prophesied some high-scoring fixtures ahead because for as many goals as we would put spectacularly in (and celebrate for ten minutes thereafter with a finger-twirling samba), they would almost instantly be nullified whenever we were next dispossessed of the ball. I remember reading in *Mr and Mrs Soccer*, Johnny Warren's account of his St George playing days,

> It was about playing with style and beauty and winning. If you won and your team played rubbishy football, the fans wouldn't speak to you. God, there was so much vitriol for an unstylish win – what a lesson that was for an Aussie kid.

I wasn't so worried about the style and beauty part with The Ladies' Men; with their spectacular hairdos and puppy-eyes, they certainly put Johnny Depp out of a job. I was more concerned about the winning part of the equation with a team concerned solely with scoring on (and off) the playing court. Defence was evidently an unnecessary chore akin to cleaning the bedroom. Dependable Tuckers would patiently toil, a solitary figure in the back line like Custer, as his pals would joyously and recklessly attack-attack-attack, leaving Wozza's goals totally exposed for counter-attack-attack-attack.

As Tuckers eloquently if not astutely pointed out with admirable self-effacement, *Not really tremendous odds, Mr Huitker. Three against one. And the one is far from the most dextrous of the side!*

I was beginning to like these little critters for the force of their collective and disparate personalities and decided to do something nice and New Age for them. I bought them all international playing tops (imitation, like their coach's) in order to convince them of my good-guy sincerity. I bought them countries and clubs which I thought matched their individual character. For instance, I gave Wozza a Dutch national team top, as there are undeniably no bigger sleeping giants in world sport; I gave Rhys an English top, as there are no bigger dreamers in world sport; and Aidan, who was an industrious, selfless workhorse, was given a Newcastle United top, a team which his family had supported for generations. We had jelly snakes after most trainings, as a nod to my mother and father's influence, and, unlike a lot of teams whom I coached in the past, the Ladies' Men could unfailingly withhold the excitement generated from their sugar-fix long enough to even thank me before they *pinged* home. So I, in turn, went home feeling warm and fuzzy. This was close to happiness and love.

I remember the Belgian coach Robert Waseige's fantastic comment that his national team needed to work on just two things – defence and attack – and grinned wryly as our final training session started with a predictable chorus of *Let's do shooting today!* Being New Age, Mark-Schwarzer-nice and slightly hippy now, I assured them we would eventually do shooting but perhaps, maybe just this once, could I have a little turn now as I was the *coach*. And would it be too much to ask if I could maybe teach them – pretty please with a cherry on top – some defensive formation? That mystical defensive pattern I appropriated from Albury...*The Box*, took me a few lunchtimes and truckloads of patience to instruct. Like me, steam blew out of their collective ears when it was first explained to them. I had forgotten to pack a ball that morning, so we used my Man. U jacket (the one which doubled as Wozza's nap blanket) tied in a spherical manner instead. So after some basic theory, I got them throwing around my clothing in an attempt to teach them zonal intricacies. My principal walked in and thought we were rehearsing a play (principals often get things terribly wrong). He mentioned something about me being resourceful, how drama games were great for bonding and told me to keep up the good work. I told him I would do my damnedest. But the boys, now sick and tired after two or three minutes of jacket hurling, demanded to play with a real ball because what we were doing was 'totally pov'. I grabbed a rogue basketball.

Remarkably, the Ladies' Men then seemed to understand the essence of what I was teaching and shifted shape with consummate ease and got behind the 'jacket' with speed and enthusiasm. Tuckers particularly took a mathematical interest in proceedings and politely helped Sundo with his geography while the other terriers did as I asked because they knew that the carrot at the end of the tunnel would be lots and lots and lots of shots on goal. I told them that shots on goal were only a small proportion of what mattered with the indoor game – the lead-up being just as crucial.

But Charlie always knew the lowdown and in his usual manner, in which everything he muttered sounded like a double entendre, said, *You gotta score to win, H!*

He gave me one of those soap-commercial smiles which make soft, trendy coaches ignore completely the detailed session plans they had been burning the midnight oil over the night before. (The sort of smile I am sure will help him notch up a considerable amount of cheap points in future years.) As Charlie came up to my knees, was terse to the point of crassness and lived miles away in the bush, I was a little unsure as to where his Johnny Deppian sophistication and cocksure swagger actually evolved from. The miracle of modern television, I figured.

OK. We'll do shooting. Besides, it's getting close to Wozza's bedtime.

Wozza, who fluctuated between the frenetic and the catatonic in a moment's notice, was already yawning. I knew it would only be a matter of time before he assumed the foetal position. Aidan and Rhys were already lost in some alternative Play Station universe in which they were being harassed by nunchuck-wielding ninjas on skateboards disguised as nuns and Al, who had gone three sentences without receiving any attention reminded me, *I've got to go to Rep training!*

I sighed and caved in to the feeling that there was not much more I could effectively do before we reached the Sunshine State.

I took a brief look at Wozza, curled up and content. Then decided to emulate him on the other bench.

The bus arrived at Sunnybank Hotel (indicating that, yes, we had arrived in Queensland) well past midnight on our first day of competition. The Living Dead emerged from the doors and stumbled, arms outstretched, into their motel rooms. Those conscious enough to remember their bags retrieved them from beneath the bus. We literally had to drag Wozza to his bed.

The next morning, I politely knocked on the Ladies' Men's door to find Sally, that human dynamo on wheels, was every bit the godsend I had predicted she would be. She had been up early – no doubt to prevent Aidan or Wozza from sleepwalking under a truck on the nearby highway – and had already found a supermarket, purchased breakfast cereal, milk and juice, organised lunches and had the boys line up their boots and shirts, shorts, shin guards and socks for pre-competition inspection. I might be wrong here, but I think she then apologised for the boots not being polished and the undies not ironed while offering me a surprise café latte and a random slice of passionfruit cheesecake which she con-jarred from behind her ear.

She really is impressive and startlingly precise in her organisation, Tuckers whispered to me.

I asked Sally if we had misplaced six-sevenths of the team but she pointed to the bathroom. I walked over and found my charges intensely sculpturing and massaging the top of their heads, making sure the slimy gel was sitting perfectly in their Home And Away hairstyles. I avoided a cheap gag about cheap points but did tell them they'd muck up all that delicate hair surgery when they eventually put their playing shirts on.

They looked at me as if I was the bearer of some earth-shattering revelation when Al, the brightest spark that morning, excitedly suggested, *We'll take our gel with us!*

Wozza was trying to work out what to wear in goals and decided to wear the Dutch national top I had given him. I didn't have the heart to tell him that wearing that orange top might tarnish him with some truly wicked voodoo curse for the rest of his life, especially if any of the games in which he was to goalkeep went to penalties. But I knew that there was some Polish blood in his family and thus figured he would have some idea about what it was like to not achieve anything significant in international sport.

Do you think we'll win, H? Rhys asked.

What's important is that we do our best and grow from the experience, I replied serenely, breathing in the eucalypt-scented air as a sparrow flitted excitedly from branch to branch in the trees above me.

Rhys called me a hippy (which is a derogatory accusation when it comes from a child) and suggested that I had taken illicit substances in the seventies. He then herded the remaining Ladies' Men into the bus for our first day of competition. With some lingering travel fatigue still evident in most of the lads, yet equipped with attacking flair and enough canisters of gel to sink a frigate, we made our way to the Cornubia Sports Complex with anticipation, conviction and perhaps a little too much expectation.

Hippy indeed.

I put *Pilot's Greatest Hits* over the bus stereo and, as the dulcet tones of Magic permeated through the speakers, I waited, perversely, for the complaints to come thick and fast as I sang deliberately at Rhys, *Never believe it's not so.*

I don't know if it was an omen or not, but our first team didn't show up – and they were a Brisbane school. Surf must have been up.

As a result, we were all bunged into one pool, and had to essentially win one match to make the play-offs for the final. Wow. This was almost easier than Albury. We had achieved three points already without having to do anything. The boys didn't seem all that perturbed (Tuckers: *That's a positive start, Mr Huitker! We'll go home with at least one win!*) and were content to kick a ball around the half-empty court. The Under 19 Girls' side were watching courtside like a bunch of big Brady Sisters. They had 'adopted' The Ladies' Men (Katie: *They're soooooooo cute, Mr H!*) and treated the boys as if they were war orphans who hadn't been hugged in years because their parents had been standing under a bomb during the blitz. The Ladies' Men, true to their name, as always, were happy to accept the attentions

215

lavished upon them (and would later inform me that cuddles from the Year 12 women did in fact constitute 'cheap points').

While all this inverse cradle-snatching was occurring, I watched the remaining teams in our sole pool slug it out on another court. Being superstitious, I had a fear of being presented with an early forfeit and the associated (cheap) three points would not place us in good stead for our second match against a flashy side from Warrigal Road. My fears were realised as I watched them clinically dispatch a fellow Brisbane side in our pool from Yugumbir. The Warrigals were led by a little blonde dude – also superbly gelled – whose goal-scoring prowess was often celebrated with that familiar scorer's samba, punctuated with an index-finger wagging in overdrive. And not only was the Warrigal side well drilled, but they had an officious little man as a coach, equipped with the telltale weapon of major disquiet for all opposition coaches: a clipboard.

I owned a little reusable Snickers mini-whiteboard which someone left at a tournament one day and I had appropriated. (OK, I stole it.) The boys loved it when I used the thing because it made us look *professional*, but it didn't take long before my diagrams started to resemble the etchings on one of Russell Crowe's formulae-ridden blackboards in *A Beautiful Mind*. And then *whoosh* out flew the steam from seven pairs of pre-teen ears. As

I threw the bloody thing away one practice match, Sally, with that never-mind look of caring on her face, retrieved the orphaned mini-whiteboard and suggested the need for a follow-up coffee and cheesecake. *There, there*, she soothed.

Tuckers, who had grown tired of meaningless shooting at goals on the empty court behind us, joined me to assess the Warrigal game. After a few seconds, he said, *They'll be a somewhat difficult team to circumvent!*

I looked back at my charges. Al and Charlie were hopelessly in love with a pretty little girl from another Brisbane school team dressed in a fire-red silky playing strip – and they had begun the slow process of introducing themselves by commencing with the first stage of junior high dating: stalking. Aidan and Sundo looked satisfied in the knowledge that they were in Brisbane and knew exactly where they were. Rhys was very happy juggling a ball with some friendly local neighbourhood ninjas. But thankfully, reunification of the team occurred when Wozza discovered a toddler's play park – equipped with a mind-blowingly fun kiddie train, irresponsibly dangerous monkey bars and a sticky baby slippery-dip – adjacent to the Cornubia Sporting Complex. I guess I couldn't complain. Whenever I needed to locate them, the Ladies' Men would either be rooting for the Under 19s Girls, helplessly stalking the 'hot chick' in red or cheerfully frolicking footloose and fancy-free with five-year-olds in a ridiculous multicoloured play park under the watchful eye of a murder of adoring Brissie mums. The mums would invariably crow to me that annoying phrase which seemed to annoyingly follow these dapper boys wherever they went: *They're soooooooooo cute.*

They were The Ladies' Men after all.

Like all coaches, I hoped for points by association.

We were 3–1 up against Warrigal, and even cautious ol' H started to think the lads had it in the bag. The boys, keen to finally get on the court and sport their gel in front of a real crowd, looked great in attack. In fact, that was all they did. Attack-attack-attack. On top of this, another sorry TLM trait was starting to develop – an uncanny and unsettling ability to hit the opposition's goalpost on demand. We could have put the game well out of Warrigal's grasp on numerous occasions were it not for this supernatural skill of hitting the woodwork from even the minutest of distances.

We paid for it.

The Warrigal side was obviously not used to losing and staged an impressive three-goal fight-back to steal the game from us. The three goals naturally came when the boys had totally abandoned any defensive formation in their insatiable lust to attack-attack-attack when they were two goals ahead. Attack-attack-attack we did and when the ball hit the woodwork or we were dispossessed we suddenly found ourselves scored against-against-against.

I was as disappointed as the next (Ladies') man, but even world-weary ol' H was not ready for the scenes that ensued. Whereas my 16 Blues dismissed a loss by simply branding the opposition a pack of gay homosexuals, TLM were a little more explosive. Benches were kicked. Shirts, bags and towels went flying. Spectators, mothers and passers-by were threatened with violence. And just when I expected the boys to burst out of their ripped kits, transform into burly, hulky, cranky green men and tear the Cornubia Sports Centre apart, they all, in unison, burst, instead, into big, blubbery tears. I looked at Sally, who was quite doggedly chanting her *there-there* mantra as the universe collapsed around us, when I realised that if I didn't move my tearful tackers quickly then the court might be rendered unplayable for the next fixture due to excessive flooding. The Under 19 girls tried to console their little boyfriends but, being male and having just lost, the Ladies' Men hardly even noticed this ideal opportunity to acquire some very very easy cheap sympathy points. In fact, in consoling them in my befuddled somewhat paternal manner, I was the only one gaining any sort of points, it seemed – and only by association – from the murder of Brissie mothers and Under 19 Brady Girls who kept purring, *Oooooo, he's soooooooo good with them,* mixed in with the perennial favourite, *They're soooooooooo cute.*

We went up to what was to become our dressing room, a shady little alcove hidden in a bend halfway up the disabled access ramps at the side of the Cornubia courts. People would pass by and provide us with disabling glances of sympathy and pity, assuming, naturally, that someone we knew had recently died. Such was the all-pervading level of gloom radiating from my collection of pre-pubescent wailers. Tuckers indicated that it was still, in fact, quite mathematically possible to make the semis. And got punched.

It took nice New Age H a lot of positive, flowery energy to help negate the grave torment which had descended upon their fragile little souls. I had realised that the loss was possibly the most devastating thing that had ever occurred to them. At least for that week. And if that little red-clad vixen didn't provide any return for Al and Charlie's total dedication, I feared I might lose the team forever. I told them about plenty of fish, the sea and that it had been a close match and that we should emphatically beat the team which Warrigal had comfortably brushed aside earlier in the day if I had any idea what I was talking about.

That renewed some confidence and halted an irksome dose of sniffling but, as usual, I had opened my mouth far too wide. All the inroads made by my holistic, hand-holding group therapy session came asunder when we lost, 4–3 again, in the next match. (If I am ever looking like being involved in a 4–3 fixture, get me miles away from the match quickly. Any team I am associated with will be laboured with the 3 bit of the scoreline. I tell you, it's as certain as sundown.) Once more, we hit the post with professional dexterity, over-committing in attack-attack-attack and allowing a weaker opposition to get on top of us when all we had to do was defend – just occasionally – with more than one player.

This time, it was as if someone had disconnected all the pipes at the waterworks and turned the water-pressure to 11. The rage portion of the PMS (Post Match Sulk) lasted even longer this time as the utter disbelief that we had lost a *second* game sunk in after the ref's whistle. I didn't really know where to look as seven lethal little twisters of frustration were wreaking unmerry havoc on inanimate objects all around them. I suggested that spectators make for the cellars.

While Al kept muttering how we played like excrement, Charlie had picked up his wallet and decided he needed to hurl it at something big and solid. Driven by his rage, he scanned to his left and right but, realising the partitions separating the courts were made of rope and plastic (and hence too flimsy), he headed, blood-red, towards the back wall of the indoor arena. By the time he got to the wall, his rage had subsided somewhat (it's a long walk for a twelve-year-old), but, realising that others were watching him, he deduced that he had to finish the cranky action he had begun. So he hurled the wallet, somewhat half-heartedly, at the wall. It went *pthwerrrt*, like a languid fart, seeming to stick there for an eternity before dropping with a quickness akin to birdshit rapidly descending onto a newly-cleaned car window. From a very high branch.

I took my crying posse back to the bend on the disabled ramp (with the posse now consisting of Sally, The Brady Bunch sisters and Brisbane mums all giving me that loving, understanding and admiring there-there look with the odd *Oooooo, he's soooo good with them* thrown in, again, for good measure). I kept my cool but, the more New Age and nice I got, the more they cried. The more I patted them on the head, the greater the tap leaked. (They didn't even admonish me for interfering with the gel.) The more I gave them reassuring big-brotherly punches, the more they seemed to doubt my geeky ability to appease them in any meaningful way. The more I suggested that maybe, perhaps maybe, an eeny-weeny attempt at trying my defensive formation might help them secure a win, the more they looked at me as though I was a used car salesman on stilts. There followed an even bigger burst of bawling when Al asserted that we were in fact excrement and our future in the competition looked like excrement and there was no hope of making the excremental finals.

However, Tuckers indicated that it was still quite mathematically possible to make the semis.

And got punched, once again, on cue.

In our third game we were down by one goal at half-time. This pre-empted the R&T (Rage and Tear) Fest well before the game was even over.

Keep centred, H, I said to myself. *They need you to be level-headed here. Anger is a useless emotion – let it fly free, like a dove. Like an ever-opening flower. All you need is love. Remember, Bondi United Under 12s. The ideals. The dreams.*

And then, one of the little charmers spat out, *YOU SAID WE'D MAKE THE FINAL, H...!* Laced with an unhealthy amount of vitriol, shittiness and accusation, I'm afraid this sentence broke the cranky dam inside me. The boys were all looking up at me through angry tears as if I had promised them a pony for Christmas and hadn't come up with the goods. Heck, there arrives that point in every man's life when 'genoeg is genoeg' (Dutch for enough is enough) – when the softly-spoken, earth-loving Mark-Schwarzer-of-the-soul can take no more and disappears to the coast for a surf. Dusk had now well and truly arrived across the cloudy horizon of the New Age. It was now about to piss down.

I recalled Alex Ferguson saying in his autobiography, *Managing My Life* that 'managers earn their wages in the ten or fifteen minutes they spend with their men at halftime'. Well, I was about to earn me some money. I warned Sally, who was standing by my side, that things were about to get ugly. She nodded knowingly.

GET IN HERE AND GET IN HERE NOW!

Reputable sources inform me that I was heard five suburbs away.

The boys assembled with the speed of a *ping*. Sally stood a few metres away, still with a knowing look on her face which suggested that she had expected Volcano

224

Huitker to erupt at any point now anyway. I could see this saintly woman was thinking caffeine and cheesy patisserie.

But no cheesecake was going to hold me back this time.

THE NEXT PERSON WHO SHEDS A TEAR WILL NOT PLAY FOR THE REST OF THE SERIES. (Luckily, the fact that the ensuing game would most likely have been our last one had escaped them.) *NOW SIT DOWN, FIX YOUR EYES ON ME AND GIVE ME YOUR UNDIVIDED ATTENTION FOR THE NEXT TWO MINUTES.* (At this point, I went back to lower-case ranting.) *I did not give up all my time for training sessions followed up with a nineteen-hour bus trip to coach A BIG BUNCH OF CRY-BABIES!* (Occasionally I will revert back to uppercase for emphasis.) *I can understand you being disappointed in those first games because you did a couple of nice things in attack-attack-attack. BUT WHAT DO YOU EXPECT IF YOU DON'T DEFEND? In brief, the opposition will always score more than you – no matter how many times you go for glory or how TOTALLY UNFAIR it is that you hit the post fifty times in a game. There's no such thing as karma in sport. I can understand you being disappointed, but crying halfway through a bloody game that's not even bloody finished yet is simply bloody SISSY. If you try your best and lose, I can excuse a sniffle or two here and there, but I WILL NOT EVER IN A MILLION YEARS LET YOU COME OFF BEFORE A GAME IS FINISHED AND HAVE YOU BLUBBING BECAUSE YOU HAVEN'T WON IT. For Mr Miyagi's sake, boys, IT'S NOT OVER YET! I can accurately predict this much, though – if you don't stop howling and wailing and dummy-spitting, and start fighting back and defending – LIKE I COACHED YOU – I'm going to herd us all on the bus right now and tell Barry The Bus Driver to take us back home.* (The one good thing about little kids is that they believe idle threats.) *And listen to me carefully...* (I eyed every one of them for maximum effect, nearly causing them to cry again) *I DO NOT CARE IF YOU LOSE – BUT I DO CARE IF YOU DO NOT TRY. While at Coventry City, Gordon Strachan said that he could accept players having a bad day if they played honestly. But you are playing DIS-HON-EST-LY.* (Isolating syllables is a very effective tool in power speeches.) *NOW GET OUT THERE AND SCORE SOME GOALS, HAVE FUN, DON'T DUMMY-SPIT AND JUST FOR ONCE SHOW ME SOME ZONE DEFENCE SO THAT I CAN FEEL I'VE CONTRIBUTED EVEN IN A SMALL WAY TO THIS WHOLE SORRY DEBACLE OF A TOUR.* (Pause.) *GO!*

They *pinged* out onto the field – all seven of them – and I had to hold two of them back to sub. I noticed players on the other court who had heard my speech were also still quaking with a strange mixture of fear and inspiration. I asked Sally if I had gone too far. She shook her head and said, *About bloody time.*

We lost the game, but this time there were no tears on the disabled ramp. Tuckers did make the point that making the final was still mathematically possible.

226

No longer New Age, this time I decided to punch him myself.

No, I thought, *that's not fair.* I shouldn't take my frustrations out on the team brain. That always happens, nastily, in teen comedies. I should check the tables myself.

Then punch him.

To my disbelief, my little team strategist was in fact correct. Due to unusual results in the other games and despite losing three on the trot, TLM could still make the finals if they could beat Yugumbir by more than they had beaten us the first time. Essentially, we had to win by two goals to get through. Scoring the goals would not be an issue, as Yugumbir had defensive frailties. The challenge would be to keep *them* from scoring.

We had a team meeting in the hotel room upon returning and I announced that I knew how they could advance to the final but wouldn't tell them because they were a pack of cry babies and never listened to a word I said. As my hero Gordon Banks wrote in his autobiography, 'One of the problems with coaching is that you can only teach those willing to learn.' I petulantly told them they were in with a mathematically good chance all week to make the final due to their close losses (giving Tuckers a wink), but as they were too busy chucking tantrums I felt they couldn't really do anything substantial about improving their chances.

Tell us and stop being a dick! Al challenged.

Yeah! yelled the others.

I'll think about it, I calmly replied, *and we'll have a team meeting tonight at 6.30 to talk about it. No, better make that 5.30, or we'll lose Wozza.* I pretended to walk out of the room then said, *Oh and I've been meaning to do this all week...*

I grabbed Al in a headlock and messed up his hair and before he could call me an excrement-tete I had Wozza under my weight and was mercilessly messing the gel on his head as well. I was a man who had been pushed too far. I would wreak my revenge on the whole village. As I finished with Wozza, I was heading for Rhys – and a truckload of invisible ninja pals of his – when TLM, to a man, jumped me.

It was my first ever team brawl.

I had, proudly, messed up pretty much everyone's hair

until Charlie inadvertently kneed me in the balls and that was the end of that. Vulnerable and squeaking in pain as I was, the rest of The Ladies' Men took advantage of my agonised state, grabbed their pillows and pummelled me into oblivion. As I disappeared beneath a mass of flying feathers, I heard Sally at the door...

Stop that at once or it will be lights out first thing after dinner!

The mass disentangled and Sally had to double-take when she noticed me at the bottom. Grinning through clenched teeth in a defeated clump on the hotel floor was the New Age, hippy, peace-loving, Mark-Schwarzer-nice coach, one hand trying to block out the afternoon light shining through the doorway. The other shielding a pair of ruptured testicles. Once more, I wasn't too sure how this all looked to neutral observers.

They fight dirty, I said in a high-pitched Bee Gees voice, nodding down at my goolies. But by the time we had found some ice to reduce the swelling, the lads were already in the bathroom fixing their hair.

I hope we're sufficiently bonded, said Sally.

That night at the hotel, I resurrected the Snickers whiteboard and returned to my penchant for Russell Crowe squiggles. I even quoted from *A Beautiful Mind* where John Nash tells his mates in a bar that 'the best result will come from everyone in the group doing what's best for himself and the group'. In my humble opinion, we would need to anchor two of our solid players in the back line and these players were to resist the allure of scoring heroics and hold a tight defensive line at the back of...*The Box*.

...*The Box*, whispered back my team, hushed and reverently.

I suggested that Aidan and Al play at the back of...*The Box* and for once received no argument from TLM. I repeated five or six times that they were not to depart from the back of...*The Box* under any circumstances and to leave the scoring to Charlie, Rhys, Tuckers and Sundo. I promised them that if they stuck to this formation they would not be beaten and I would honour their wish of making the final. We all let out a cheer like a bunch of pirates on a brig and I remembered that I had every intention of taking them, as promised, to see *The Pirates of the Caribbean* that night after dinner. But with possibly two big games the next day and most of the team yawning profusely, Sally vetoed that idea and sent the cabin boys (and me) back to our hammocks. I said to her that I was sorry if I had been too aggro with them earlier today and promised her I would go back to being New Age and nice for the semi-final.

But I could tell by that maternal, all-knowing roll of her eyes that she knew I couldn't be anything but myself.

The 'unofficial' semi-final turned out to be an anticlimax, the boys easily accounting for Yugumbir, winning convincingly 5–1. While being characteristically flamboyant in attack, the opposition simply were outclassed by Aidan's and Al's defence, with Rhys, Tuckers, Charlie and Sundo rising to the occasion in attack-attack-attack. Yugumbir began taking shots from further out, which Wozza, wide awake, effortlessly dealt with. But this game was Al's, who had a blinder, putting his advanced footwork to full effect against a baffled opposition.

I had a sudden urge to dress up for the final. If we were playing at home in Canberra, I would have changed our name to the Radford Pirates and got dressed up like Johnny Depp. This might have served to cheer up Al and Charlie, who were having no success with that pretty Brisbane girl and had now got in far too deep by making up saucy imaginary conversations which they had apparently had with her (when in fact they had simply stalked her from a distance of three hundred metres for most of the preceding day). Cheap points would be hard to collect if saying *Hello* was such a big deal. The Under 19 girls offered to help keep the pointage clocked up, but I requested that they save their energy to cheer us on if we made the final.

Anyway, having not seen *Pirates of the Caribbean* as yet, I decided to adopt an over-confident happy-go-lucky swashbuckling yet cynical attitude to the day's events, as I figured that would make a nice contrast to my clinical little clipboard-wielding counterpart. (I could imagine that, while we were spending our pre-final time world series wrestling, the Warrigal boys were probably assimilating pages and pages of graphs of complex set plays until steam came out of their poor little ears.)

Sucko, I thought, no longer a nice guy. *Pirates aren't meant to take prisoners.*

Pirates are mean.

We had just won the Under 19 Boys and Under 14

Girls titles and I knew that good things came in threes, although it would be a pretty rare thing for a school to win three national titles one after the other. Unfortunately, for reasons again beyond me, TLM were rescheduled as the last final to be played no later than 5.30 p.m. My biggest fear was that Wozza would fall asleep halfway through the game and I knew intuitively that we couldn't afford our goalkeeper to remain horizontal, snoring, for the duration of the match.

But the good thing was that all four remaining Radford teams would be on hand to cheer on The Ladies' Men, who certainly responded to any sort of affirmation, if not the odd critical lambasting. The lads were certainly buoyed by the Under 19 Boys' win, against all odds in a very tough senior competition, a win coach Jann dedicated to her father, Jack; and then the Under 14 Girls, coached by my friend Rufus (who I believe had never touched an indoor ball in his life prior to the Nationals and indeed believed that futsal was a debilitating fungal disease) came from nowhere to win their final as well. Was it possible that the tide was turning our little Radford way?

Aidan's father, Paul, had overheard the possibly over-confident Warrigal boys discussing the ensuing final. *We scored four against them the first time, five in the second match. This time it's going to be six!* I can remember thinking, *Had they taken the time to watch our game against Yugumbir, they might have been better prepared for our change in playing style.* So I lived somewhat comforted in the knowledge that our brand-new approach, formation and strategy had not found its way onto the exhaustive clipboard of the Warrigal coach.

The Ladies' Men started strongly. In fact, we scored the first goal. Charlie and Rhys were being creative in attack-attack-attack and, when given our first clear chance, Charlie scored the first of two of the most important points on tour. I remember hearing Aidan and Al reinforcing to each other to *Keep The Box – Maintain The Box – Trust in The Box.* I felt strangely Jedi myself, reminding my competitive, jackal side of the brain to look behind the grand final, realise and release the potential of these boys and not be seduced by the hint of success.

And then Warrigal came for us.

The onslaught was unrelenting as wave after wave of attacking opposition play bombarded TLM's goal area. I started to have severe doubts about...*The Box* and was wondering when its cardboard exterior would be exposed for what it truly was – something I had once stolen from another guy in Albury who sounded as though he knew what he was doing. But Charlie and Rhys did all they could to get behind play instead of sitting in the opposition's half waiting for a hopeful rogue ball to spill their way while leaving our defences exposed. Al and Aidan were showing admirable restraint, trusting their forwards and resisting the temptation to express themselves in attack-attack-attack – doing what was best for the team more so than what might be good for their individual selves.

But the game was Wozza's, whose goalkeeping not only defied gravity but logic as well. I remember reading England's World Cup winning 'keeper, Gordon Banks suggesting that

> ...the mark of a good goalkeeper is how few saves he has to make in a game. A spectacular save is the last resort when all else – positioning, anticipation, defence – have failed. But saves are always what we are remembered for.

But as Warrigal started to deploy missiles from out wide, where...*The Box* was pushing their play, the shots on target were calling for nothing short of the spectacular from Wozza. Usually this would not concern me, but the front Warrigal pairing had strong, cannonball shots and they were starting to hone their radar from out wide. Yet whenever they did, Wozza, with a strange 'keeping style of equal parts Astroboy and Jet Li – and informed by the aerodynamics from all of those lunchtime dwarf-throwing sessions – would throw himself theatrically at every missile fired at every corner of his goal. In his orange Netherlands top, he became the Flying Dutchman (from Poland), each save more spectacular and memorable than the last. And, in keeping with the theatrics of the situation, Wozza would turn to the Radford crowds in the stands (who now outnumbered the home state's supporters by 379 to five) and conduct their enthusiastic chanting with rotating hands and spirit fingers while strutting in a circle like Mick Jagger on steroids. It had the desired effect, inspiring an almost rabid crescendo from the Radford cheerleaders, ably led by Marcia, Jan and Cindy.

By halftime, we were sensing a boil-over. Johnny Warren's view 'that the best coaches have the ability to alter the course of a game at half-time' kept restating itself in my mind. I noticed that the Warrigal coach was frantically drawing lines on his clipboard while maintaining that clinical calm that I find so bloody annoying in psychologists, religious zealots and the truly competent. I saw my Snickers board protruding from the kitbag and felt, for a moment, the urge to draw it to me like a security blanket and frenetically etch on it lots of squiggles of intent designed to display my intricate understanding of the workings of this pressure match.

But when it came down to it, I knew they would only be the etchings of hope. In my head, I now heard a little voice reciting a quotation by British playwright Steven Berkoff, 'rely on nothing but your own imagination and good will of your fellow players. Risk all, since you will not die when it's over.' And yes, I felt my imagination and TLM's goodwill would be enough. Next a strange mix of images from all those Hollywood Bs flooded my brain in a sort of MTV mega image-mix.

> You're in need of a miracle – these kids aren't old enough to drink yet, chortled Coach Morris Buttermaker. Trust in the heart and mind, murmured Mr Miyagi. The Force is strong in these young ones, uttered Yoda. Do it for Mickey Goldmill – he was like a father to me, sobbed Rocky. First you played for respect and now you're playing against the world, warned Gordon Bombay. Before they can win, they have to become one, hissed Herman Boone. Your team's a small town on the outskirt of greatness, encouraged a butt-naked team of Alaskan ice hockey players. And be a nice guy! advised Mark Schwarzer (who actually had no career in film as yet) surrounded by a bunch of Under 12s with soccer balls and surfboards.

If there's one thing fairytale sports films can provide you with, it is sufficient inspiration to believe in the possibility of somehow winning, even through loss, in those moments of self-doubt. And how could anyone argue that that is a bad thing? I turned to The Ladies' Men United – for now I finally fully understood why teams put that at the end of their club names – and said with that cracker guitar solo from Pilot's 'Magic' playing behind in the soundtrack in my head,

I'm not going to change a thing, boys. Let's trust, rely and believe in this shape – on what we've worked on. We trust in Wozza in goal; we rely on our backs to hold their formation; we believe our forwards will be imaginative enough to score against a team that is capable of breaking down even the most creative of attacks – like the Borg. And we should have faith that our subs will be able to carry on with the mission. Warrigal are a more lethal team than us in attack-attack-attack, but that's not everything in sport. We need to work on two things, remember – attack AND defence. (Bless you, Robert Waseige.) *So let's not give them a sniff. Hold them out and we'll ping them in the counter-attack – which is what they've been doing to us and all the other teams all week: waiting for us to over-commit and then scoring a sucker punch. Sometimes you've got to beat the opposition at their own game and sucker-punch them back. YOU UP TO IT?*

Tuckers informed he was too busy to play. He would prefer sitting on the bench manipulating the match statistics, checking the charts and running the computers. I turned to Sundo and said I would try to get him out in the final stages of the game. He nodded, a little nervously, then resumed his seat next to mine as the boys ran out for their final twenty minutes together as The Ladies' Men.

The Radford contingent roared like lions.

I stole a glance at the Warrigal coach, cradling his clipboard close to his chest with commendable self-assurance and centredness. One day, I thought, I might develop that sort of inner peace in the face of adversity. In a strange way, he actually was my hero more than my antagonist.

But for now I decided to join our supporters and try to yell our boys over the line.

With absolutely no peace in my soul.

Wozza pulled off spectacular save after spectacular save. The crowd, directly above and behind him in the stands for the second half, lifted his confidence to intoxicating heights. Being a 'keeper who sometimes wore a Netherlands top myself in a past life, I was warmed by all this, remembering again my hero Gordon Banks's cautionary words that 'it's no good performing heroics for eighty-nine minutes if you lose concentration for a second and give away a silly goal'. Surely the gods would not be that cruel?

Meanwhile, the Warrigal attack, remaining unrelenting in its resolve, became increasingly frustrated. Aidan and

Al worked as an aggressive duo like those two sharks in *Deep Blue Sea* while Charlie and Rhys – who fought and defended like Batman and Robin – were starting to create larger openings in the opposition defence in which to explore and exploit. Then, as if scripted, with very little time left on the clock, Charlie found himself in a little space and effortlessly slotted the ball past the Warrigal 'keeper, and in doing so broke the back of the plucky, previously undefeated opposing side. I tried to sub Sundo on for Rhys – who had played his heart out and was fatiguing – but in the madding din and chanting of the 379 Radford fans in the stands (let me hear you clap your hands), Rhys couldn't hear my call for a sub.

And even with precious seconds left on the clock, the Ladies' Men maintained their shape...*The Box*. Now more than metaphorically...*The Box* became impenetrable, allowing no hint of an opportunity for the Warrigal warriors to successfully raid or even make a peep-hole in.

When the referee blew the final whistle, my arms shot instantly into the air. The Under 19 players, who had been gathering near the court opening, rushed onto the field and lifted each of the Ladies' Men up onto their shoulders and threw them around the top of Cornubia like pizza dough.

I was so pathetically happy I could feel tears starting to well and I figured that that was all well and good as I needed to do something snaggy since ruthlessly abandoning my New Age charter. Besides, Dickens once wrote that 'we need never be shamed of our tears, for they are rain upon the blinding dust of earth, overlying our hard hearts'. And before anyone could get to me I rushed over to the opposition coach and shook his hand and said, *I'm sorry.*

And I really meant it.

For a moment there, I felt a little sick to the stomach, especially watching the Warrigal boys slowly and dejectedly packing their kitbags and hastily retreating, in sad single file, towards the exits amidst all the Radfordian commotion. In truth, that made the moment hard to enjoy, because I had been in their place so so many times before in so so many situations over so so many years. And as Emily Dickinson once whispered, 'Success is counted sweetest / By those who ne'er succeed'. I knew, even then, that I was feeling so bloody happy because the sensation of victory was such a damned rare thing for me. But just at the point when the guilt at having won started oiling up my soul (and the realisation that maybe I wasn't cut out for the art of winning gracefully), I found my arms outstretched towards the heavens once more in a big

V for Victory salute. I was celebrating relief more than anything, that's for sure, but also the unbridled joy that all these little boys in my superbly gelled team were now immersed in.

Jann was one of the first to notice me and she rushed over and gave me a huge bear hug. We looked at each other momentarily, both so desperately wanting to be sharing the elation with our respective fathers. But both of us were cluey and crazy enough to know that, if you strained your eyes slightly when looking through the misty lens at the end of sporting events, you can see your dads – along with the likes of Mickey Goldmill, Obi-Wan Kenobi and maybe even Patches O'Houlihan, sitting slightly away from all the hubbub, together on the now abandoned benches at the halfway line, smiling gently and knowingly.

Virginia Woolf stated that when a man reaches the age of thirty 'the time when he is thinking becomes inordinately long'. This is so true. I could not help but continuously mull over my feelings about TLM's unexpected win and the strange blend of elation and guilt that was attacking me as we waited for the presentation. I thought back to that quarter-final loss with the Blues when this silly futsal thing started three years ago, and wondered if I actually enjoyed painfully losing something more than actually winning anything.

The Warrigal captain, the index-finger samba now de-wagged, gave a dignified and genuine speech congratulating Radford's performance, which made me feel even worse. I was now one of the bad guys. A *winner*. And of a National Title to boot. While I felt that little blondie needed to come down a peg or two during the round matches, I hoped we hadn't totally removed the reggae from his rotations.

Hopefully we will see you again next year, he said with a winning grin, and I was happy to see, at the very least, that it was a cheeky one. You always can tell a gracious loser – the samba is still there in the smile, and the person concerned is thinking beyond the little loss and out into the big, unknowable, possible future.

I looked at the 'trophy' we were about to receive. I tried to kid myself that it was the journey that mattered but, like most men, get mercilessly seduced by these token, made-on-the-cheap mementos which get handed out at the end of things. These pathetic, disposable items can take a savage hold on you which far outstrips their relative worth.

The winner's plaque was the shape of a box.

I would not let the irony escape me as I kept reiterating in my head that this was never about winning but more about the journey. About enjoying the special, unique gifts of your fellow travellers – players and staff alike. As J.K. Rowling stated in that first Harry Potter instalment, 'There are some things you can't share without ending up liking each other, and knocking out a twelve-foot mountain troll is one of them.'

And then there's all those things you learn before encountering the troll. Sometimes you get the girl's mobile number. Other times you don't. Sometimes you hit the post and it goes in, other times it doesn't. Sometimes the best made plans of mice and men work when written on a whiteboard or clipboard, at other times it's better to wing it. Sometimes fortune approaches in steered boats, sometimes it arrives without a captain having any sense of direction at the wheel. Sometimes it's about finding the balance even as the ground beneath you shifts. You win sometimes. You lose sometimes. Two sides of the coin. Yin. Yang. That is really what sport is all about. Experiencing all those little bits of life in a (mostly) controlled environment.

I can hear you bleating sceptically, dear reader: he just wants to win as much as anyone else! It's not about *kaizen* at all. He's full of crap.

Maybe so. And maybe all I can do in reply is to grasp

helplessly at the comfort of quotation, this time by Archbishop Anthony Bloom who stated that 'the proper response to love is to accept it. There is nothing to do.' And all I could usefully do with the strange, new sensation of finally winning was to do just that. Accept it, let it blow over. Victory is short-lived, transient. So let it be those things.

I felt like asking Sally, Jann or Rufus or anyone else around Cornubia if I was a nice guy despite it all.

But I knew that they'd just tell me to keep working on it.

We were standing in the line at Movie World waiting for the *Lethal Weapon* ride. The National Title made it a hell of a lot easier to stomach all the bizarre things that this fun park was about to do to my body.

I can remember reflecting, in my queue-boredom, that sport was a lot like an amusement park ride. You have this vague notion of what might happen, but there would be unexpected thrills, turns, twists and novelties that may surprise even the seasoned fun park veteran. Once on the ride, you have a limited time in which you will either enjoy it or throw up from the anxiety. In general, the ride is best appreciated when you let your hands fly up and abandon all thoughts of losing unimportant things like your wallet, sanity or your life. Sometimes, overrated mental preparation just gets in the way.

Charlie looked up at me and admitted with uncharacteristic humility, *H, I'm shittin' me balls.*

I asked him how one exactly goes about doing that.

Then, in order to pass the time, we all did impromptu mimes and made revolting, sloppy noises (punctuated with a wet, flatulent coda) approximating the act of someone attempting to excrete their family jewels. Being a drama teacher, mine was the most graphic, creatively intense and unashamedly juvenile. An elderly couple behind us in Hawaiian shirts had this intense, concerned look which clearly indicated their feelings that a man like me should not be around children of any age.

As it turned out, Charlie kept everything in its place.

The ride wasn't as scary as it initially seemed. Hell, it was almost fun. If the truth be told, after the initial trepidation, the little roller-coaster journey was a thrill more than anything. Maybe sometimes you have to get over fear in order to mix it with the finer, more lasting emotions.

Full of confidence and equipped with all-you-can-eat fairy floss, my gang of seven little pirates and I set off looking for the next challenge.

Never believe it's not so.

Part Three
Send-Off Reports

Loreto

The crippled are pushed, prodded and dragged
past the stands of unsmiling pedlars
whose grim, plastic pietas and Ronaldo silkies
exist together without irony or tax,
through to the Piazza Madonna. I watch
as a boy is rocked by cobblestones,
his hands and head twitching beneath
his father's uncertain manoeuvring;
on towards the fascist-green doors of Santa Casa
where he will be lifted, with all the hope in the world,
under the certain, silent Black Madonna
high above and out of arm's reach
of the flaming zeal of pilgrims.
Now a stretcher, straight as a flatline
gets bumped to the front of the queue.
I escape into the dwindling light of day
where the manicured farms of Loreto, fuzzy
in the haze of white heat, present themselves
over the fortified walls, over the bronzed shoulder
of Pope Giovanni XIII. There, a bambino dances
with his plastic football. The boy's shirt,
bright and blue, brags
BAGGIO 10
as he swivels and swerves
with a pickpocket's precision before
that pious statue,
that big benevolent smile
which never leaves
        that huge, stony face.

14: Loreto

Kids crush evil in one hand.

S.K. Kelen, Kambah Pool, 2002

I've come to believe that sport delights in contrast and irony.

In 2001, while sitting in a small café inside the fortified walls of the Santa Casa, Italy, I wrote a poem called 'Loreto'. While scribbling, I watched the many passers-by, trudging down the cobbled main street towards the Piazza della Madonna, where a little baroque fountain bubbles before the centre of pilgrimage, the Sanctuario della Santa Casa. Under the great dome, inside the church, there exists an entire cottage where reputedly the Annunciation took place, where the holy family domiciled and outside of which Jesus honed his skills while playing left-back for the Nazareth Under 11s. Legend has it (as well as the Internet) that

> The simple cottage at Nazareth...was borne away by angels in 1291 as the Saracens descended on the Holy Land. It first arrived on a hill in Dalmatia. Here it stayed until the 10th of December 1292, when it was again miraculously moved, this time across the

Adriatic Sea to a laurel grove infested by bandits. Its final resting place, though, was a few miles away in the middle of a public highway on the top of the hill of Loreto. Experts in our more sceptical age now suggest that the bricks of Mary's house were brought from Palestine in the ships of the retreating Crusaders.

The cottage has been sensitively redecorated into a chapel, within which stands a replica of The Black Madonna of Loreto (originally destroyed by fire in 1921), an ebony statue known to shed tears and under which some miracles have apparently occurred.

From my vantage point, I watched a little bambino juggling a soccer ball in his Baggio shirt between the arcades of the Palazzo Apostolico, perhaps hoping his wish to become as famous and immortal as the gifted man whose number he so proudly wore might one day occur. I remember watching the boy, so full of frantic life, dancing with his football when a forlorn man passed by en route to the Sanctuario. This man carried in his arms a quadriplegic son of roughly the same age as Baggio Jr. The father had in his eyes that fervent, determined look of hope that he too might find for his child a miracle here, one which might return the joy of movement, balance and action which most kids so often take for granted.

I sat outside in a café, avoiding the pedlars selling

'miracle' souvenirs, such as glow-in-the-dark Virgin Marys and a wide array of ornamental rosary beads and crucifixes, mixed in amongst silky artificial football tops and Serie A paraphernalia. The bambino, after something close to fifty juggles, was called in by his own family and left, robbing me of the superb, live entertainment. I returned to my notebook and worked in my usual languid literary fashion for up to twenty minutes, until the man reappeared through the Sanctuario's bulky, army-green doors with his son still hanging in his weary arms. No miracle cure today.

Aside from his famous penalty miss, we are all very aware of the real Robbie Baggio's penchant for miracle goals. But I'm sure Roberto would possibly have traded most of them away if it meant that a poor immobile boy could walk again. God, I know I would. Here it was, juxtaposed once more. That bleak contrast between dreams and reality: a child who dreams that he may one day be as big as Baggio, set in stark contrast to a boy who dreams he could simply be a normal, walking, talking boy. And the reality being that neither will get their wish.

Months later, I was reminded of my afternoon in Loreto while reading George Negus's *The World from Italy: Football, Food and Politics,* in which the author discovered a sharp article by Rob Hughes, written after the Turkish earthquakes mentioned earlier in this book:

The image leaves a lasting impression. In a Reuters photograph, a boy maybe three years of age is rapt in child's play. Elegantly balanced, eyes on the ball, his right foot kicking it; this is the figure of the innocence and sheer fun of soccer. In the background is a jumble of belongings in a Turkish tent camp days after the earthquake. It might also temper the hype, the cant, the nationalism aroused by the same game.

The infant's ability to find distraction in a ball is a reminder what power, what joy the game holds... See that it is a gift, a joy, an escape from the depressing side of life to be blessed with talent some people pay millions for.

Once more, the joy of sport superimposed against the harshness of life presented a striking contrast. It reminds us that sport serves, for most of us, as a pleasant distraction and momentary escape from reality. It may not be a life-changing force; as suggested by this book, I prefer to see sport as a life-*affirming* force.

For neither of the boys at Loreto, nor those in Turkey, did winning play any part in the unadulterated joy which a sporting action can provide. Unhindered by spectators, the child is allowed to lose himself in the moment, free himself of time and align himself with his dreams while developing his skills through a joyous act. It is a sad question to ask, but how often does this happen for kids on training parks and match days in your junior league? And how much of a part do the spectators play in tainting this joyous act? Ironically, in juggling for sheer joy, the child is possibly taking a minuscule step towards achieving those larger, wilder dreams. Through this simple and joyous act of repetition, he can improve his skills and, if done regularly and with love, take that tiny step closer to realising the dream. Every one of our sports idols did it when they were kids against back walls, in backyards and in rehearsal rooms. I am fond of quoting to my various teams Alex Ferguson's description of that other famous penalty-misser David Beckham's willingness to embrace repetition:

> When footballers complain about the dullness of repetitive passing exercises it is usually not monotony they resent but hard work. David Beckham is Britain's finest striker of a football not because of God-given talent but because he practises with a relentless application that the vast majority of less gifted players wouldn't contemplate. Practise may not make you perfect but it will definitely make you better and any player working with me on the training ground will hear me preach the virtue of repetition – repeatedly.

But, as indicated already, hard work, whether it is enjoyable or otherwise, does not necessarily mean you will get to realise your ambitions.

Bobby Charlton labelled Old Trafford (Manchester United's home ground) as 'The Theatre Of Dreams'. I've always found that name fascinating. 'Theatre' is after all associated with artifice, dry ice and greasepaint while 'dreams' can conjure images of something intangible, untenable, misty. For the players in the middle of the Old Trafford pitch, it may well be the realisation of a childhood dream, but the reality for the remaining tens of thousands in the stands is that they have to live vicariously through the players below. This means investing, along with their energies, in a pricey season ticket in order to feel that they too are a small part of whatever glorious or inglorious action occurs down there most weekends. All this seems so far removed from the children that they all once were, actually playing and doing something when juggling in the backyard for free.

And this is where sport becomes painful. As a spectator, you become further distanced from physically participating in the game you love. You fill this void sometimes by engaging in other peripheral concerns such as screaming, shouting and fighting. Or by living vicariously through your children. Yet despite how much money you pay, how many backs you scratch and allegiances you switch, sport does not always play ball. In stadiums as huge as Old Trafford or as mini as your children's Roo-ball parks, you begin to place onto players/children your own sense of wish fulfilment which is often misguided and centred on winning and success and dollar signs. And all based on the *possibility* of a good result. Hell, life is tough enough as it is, so if you can't totally win and succeed and get value for money in your real-life pursuits, then hopefully there is a chance we can do so in our theatre of dreams? Right?

Yet what goes on in the centre, that seeming manifestation of our desire for the individual to succeed and to survive against all the odds, is a tenuous thing. Events do not always go as planned. And you recognise, more and more so with each game, that you have less control over them than you wish. Hence it's a bloody shame that people can work themselves up into pain, strokes, violence and even murder because of them – particularly *sporting* events. It's a shame they lose friends because of them. It's a shame they forget about lasting things such as allegiance, development and the pure joy of playing *because* events don't go according to the script.

For elite sportspeople, the game is more than just a distraction or an escape from reality. They spend their life trying to manipulate game situations so that events work for them. It has become their reality, their job, their life, their lifeblood. But these are such a small percentage – 0.0000088%. In these days where the serious side of sport is given far too much prominence

– and this seriousness is creeping into our junior leagues worldwide – we must emphatically fight the urge for sport to become anything more than a joyous distraction and healthy escape from the occasional or regular bitterness of reality. Which is why we must challenge the parents with no ideas, the coaches from hell, the bloodthirsty supporters, and systems, organisations and academies that encourage kids, parents and coaches to think like ruthless professionals before they've even signed a contract, seen a cent or let their kids finish soiling their nappies. All of these unhealthy people and their silly, stupid, serious systems return us back to the heavy, gooey reality we should be escaping from.

Let the kid juggle freely and happily.

With unadulterated joy.

S/he need not and probably will not be the next world champion. It is as unlikely as finding a miracle cure in a small Italian chapel. As improbable as stepping out onto the hallowed turf of Old Trafford. So let 'em play not to change their lives but to affirm them. I repeat Socceroo Harry Williams's wise words that we should keep things in perspective:

> In the end, it is just a sport and I am not sure that people should be remembered for being good at a sport.

The good thing is, for most of us clumsy, backyard jugglers of joy, there is always next season. Most of us are happy that we have another chance to compete for success (in the narrow person's perspective) or continual development (in the more enlightened) whenever we engage in sport. So unless our injury is physically or mentally paralysing, we will survive to try again next year.

And seeing if all that joyous juggling has paid off.

Theatre and sport, my two passions, are more closely linked than one would initially imagine. Any one of the coaches in the What Coach Is That? module could just as easily have been substituted for directors or actors. In trying to explain my obsession (or addiction) to both, I was drawn by two passages in David Mamet's *Three Uses of the Knife*. In one instance, he likens sport to a dramatic solution, in that it

> ...stands for the ability of the individual to triumph. The true drama, and especially the tragedy, calls for the hero to exercise will, to create, in front of us, on the stage, his or her own character, the strength to continue. It is her striving to understand, to correctly assess, to face her own character (in her choice of

battles) that inspires us – and gives the drama power to cleanse and enrich our own character.

And through sport, and in writing this book, I have come to realise that making sense of my obsession with coaching has led me to a more profound understanding, assessment and realisation of my own character while allowing me the chance to cleanse myself of many demons, foibles and failings. Through an embracement of the concept of *kaizen*, I hope I can have a better influence on my charges than I have been in times past. Or looking at it more cynically, have less of a negative effect on those who become a part of my Saturday arvo compulsion. And I trust that you, dear reader, can too.

Speaking of compulsion, when discussing gambling, Mamet astutely continues,

They gamble neither to win or lose but to maintain equilibrium… When they win, these gamblers cannot explain to themselves why they continue. If they gambled for wealth, why does wealth not please them? When they, inevitably lose, they cannot explain why they gambled in the first place – if it was for wealth, why couldn't they see the inevitable end was loss? Either result is unbearable, and so these gamblers must retreat to the compulsion, and surrender to illogic and pain to protect themselves against revelation.

And this, to me, is the same with chasing, hunting and defining winning as the sole source of success. Like gambling, it can lead to a lot of self-delusion and remove you further away from the things that truly matter in sport and life. I guess I would have some idea about all this because I'm as delusional and myopic as the next man. Or woman.

I've frequently been seduced by the compulsion of 'playing to win'. I'm prone to wallow in the raw aches and pains associated with surrendering to that illogical and unlikely truth that winning consistently and getting to the top is quite achievable, realistic, desirable and all-encompassing. But as a friend recently said to me, *Only a very small few get to know what it's like at the top, George.*

The rest of us have to look for something equally as good.

15: How To Succeed Without Winning

Bloody coach is gettin' stuck into the kids, tellin' 'em they're useless and playin' like crap and at no point in his halftime bloody speech does he tell 'em what to bloody do to stop playin' like crap...

Unidentified Parent, Sidelines, last weekend

I figure that I had better give some practical answers to the book's title. Here goes...

The Art of Sporting: His (Far From) Holiness George Huitker's 17.5 Steps Towards Contentment and Fulfilment On Match Days

1) Remember to stay happy. Sport has enough constipation associated with it as it is. It need not be life and death – sort those issues out away from the sportsfields. If you don't enjoy it, it's hardly recreation. Note that if you think sport is more than recreation you are heading into dangerous waters. Monitor yourself.

2) Remember that the people who have just beaten you in a measly game are not that much better or

bigger in the grander scheme of things. They will eventually get beaten when they move out of the small pool into the larger one with bigger, nastier, niftier fish. (South American ponds are particularly scary.) When they come back to the small pool, it will be with scars.

3) Remember to look *behind* a result. There is always something immensely valuable to be gained from even the smallest or hugest loss. You generally learn more from losses than you do from wins. Loss is a wonderful mechanism for keeping us all honest as well. Loss – and coping with it – is an integral part of the game ... and life. So if you are in a Superteam and spending too much energy trying to avoid loss (by recruiting better players or just quitting) rather than gaining in skills, strategy and character – both your own and your team's – then something will bite you in the bum very shortly.

4) Remember that if you have a son/daughter in a team or you are involved in representative circles or academy programs you will lose a certain amount of objectivity and perspective when coming to terms with success or the lack of it. Talk regularly with someone outside of your chosen sport. Ask them frequently if you've lost the plot.

5) Remember that the truly successful know how to win with high degrees of humility and grace. A loser is someone who calls someone else a loser.

6) Remember that you can be champions without winning anything. You just need to redefine and

reframe what you are setting out to achieve in more realistic goals.

7) Remember that to be an astute analyst of *why you are not succeeding* at something can be a more valuable trait than being an avid listener to *why you are succeeding*. As Norman Vincent Peale wrote in *The Power of Positive Thinking*, 'Most people would rather be ruined by praise than saved by criticism.'

8) Remember always to keep things in perspective. When feeling sorry for yourself because of sport simply do a charitable, selfless activity (preferably with teammates) for those less fortunate. Your mental attitude at the following fixture will have improved tenfold because you'll feel better about yourself for helping others. If a team engages in a charitable act together, they will be more cohesive and unified as a result.

9) Remember Mary Oliver's maxim that the real work is to look and listen. The sweet stuff of life will then naturally follow.

10) Remember to stay with your club. When things are going wrong in your life, you need your friends to be there for you. Similarly, clubs need their members to do something significant for them when at crisis points rather than whinge, complain, tantrum, pontificate and quit in a big fat huff, without even slightly attempting to solve the problem/s. Clubs, like people, deserve a second chance. Give them that much.

11) Remember not to complain without doing something about it. Instead, coach/manage a team yourself, get a referee's badge and officiate at a few games whenever you can, or do some late-night reading/research on how to improve skills, defence, attack and so on and share it with the coach. Gain an understanding of the finer points of the offside rule. Otherwise shut your big fat mouth.

12) Remember that the messages you provide throughout a junior player's sporting life can govern, influence and change the sort of player and person they become. Set a good example so that when a youngster develops grey matter they will remember you fondly.

13) Speaking of grey matter, remember that Eric Cantona once said, 'When the seagulls follow the trawler, it is because they think sardines will be thrown into the sea.' David Beckham desired his kids to be christened, but wasn't sure into which religion. Stuart Pearce spoke of the carrot at the end of the tunnel. Alan Shearer once bragged that nobody could accuse him of giving one hundred per cent at every game. Sigh. We need to provide for our kids heroes and role models who have nothing to do with professional sport. Sport professionals are generally too driven by success and focused on themselves to say anything remotely wise, sensible, sensitive, intelligent or lasting.

14) Remember that Gregory Peck believed that 'it takes ten pictures to make a star'. Significant

development and improvement will come with experience, rarely within one or two seasons. So forget about short-term achievements if you want success to be anything more than temporal.

15) Remember that it is better to be remembered as a person than as a player. It is better to be remembered for deeds rather than for antics. Be noteworthy rather than notorious.

16) Remember that success has very little to do with victory, except in a temporal sense. It has everything to do with accurately defining happiness, making correct and humane choices, embracing a kaizen philosophy of development and living your sporting and non-sporting lives with consideration for things other than your own raw and aching needs.

17) Remember to play to affirm your life rather than change it. Juggle for joy. Not for a contract.

17.5) Now who's for a round of *If You're Happy and You Know It Clap Your Hands*...??? One, two, three...

16: Bibliography

Books

Adams, Tim. *Being John McEnroe*, London: Yellow Jersey Press, 2003.

Alves, Stan. *Sacked Coach*, Melbourne: Crown Content, 2002.

Banks, Gordon. *Banksie*, London: Penguin, 2002.

Beckham, David. *My Life*, London: Collins Willow, 2003.

Berkoff, Steven. *Free Association*, London: Faber & Faber, 1996.

Best, George. *Scoring at Halftime*, London: Random House, 2003.

Cascarino, Tony. *Full Time*, Great Britain: Scribner / Townhouse, 2002.

Charlesworth, Ric. *The Coach*, Sydney: Macmillan, 2001.

—. *Shakespeare the Coach*, Sydney: Pan, 2004.

—. *Staying at the Top*, Sydney: Pan, 2002.

Dalai Lama. *The Art of Living*, London: Thorsons Press, 2001.

Dengate, John. *Attracting Birds to your Garden in Australia*, Sydney: New Holland, 1977.

Dickens, Charles. *Great Expectations*, 1861.

Dickinson, Emily. *Poems*, New Jersey: Castle Books, 2002.

267

Evans, Hugh. *Stone of the Mountain*, Melbourne: Lothian Books, 2004.

Evening Standard Sports Writers. *Sporting Spite!: Rebels and Rebellion in World Sport*, London: Ward Lock, 1991.

Ferguson, Alex. *Managing My Life*, London: Coronet, 2000.

Fischer, Tibor. *Under the Frog*, London: Vintage, 1992.

Foster, John. *Football Fever: Poems About Football*, Oxford: Oxford University Press, 2000.

Harper, Andy. *Mr and Mrs Soccer*, Sydney: Random House, 2004.

King, Stephen. *On Writing*, Great Britain; Hodder & Stoughton, 2000.

Leaming, Barbara. *Marilyn Monroe*, London: Orion Books, 1998.

Mamet, David. *Three Uses of the Knife: On the Nature and Purpose of Drama*, London: Methuen, 1998.

McCartney, Jason. *After Bali*, South Melbourne: Lothian Books, 2003.

Milstead, David. *The Big Book of Sports Insults*, London: Weidenfeld and Nicolson, 2004.

Negus, George. *The World From Italy: Football, Food and Politics*, Sydney: Harper & Collins, 2001.

Oliver, Mary. *The Leaf and the Cloud*, USA: Da Capo Press, 2000.

Parkinson, Michael. *On Football*, Great Britain: Hodder & Stoughton, 2001.

Pierre, DBC. *Vernon God Little*, London: Faber & Faber, 2003.

Rowling, J.K. *Harry Potter and the Philosopher's Stone*, London: Bloomsbury, 1997.

Saul, John Ralston. *On Equilibrium*, Penguin:
Victoria, 2001.

Solly, Ross. *Shoot Out: The Passion and the Politics
of Soccer's Fight for Survival in Australia*, Sydney:
Wiley Books, 2004.

Stam, Jaap. *Head to Head*, Great Britain: Collins
Willow, 2001.

Tutu, Desmond. *No Future Without Forgiveness*, New
York: Doubleday, 1999.

Warren, Johnny. *Sheilas, Wogs and Poofters : An
Incomplete Biography of Johnny Warren and Soccer in
Australia* (3rd edn), Sydney: Random House, 2003.

Wallace, Neil Montagnana. *Our Socceroos*, Sydney:
Random House, 2004.

Woolf, Virginia. *Orlando*, London: Vintage Classics, 1928.

Internet

ABC On-Line. 'I Won't Quit Captaincy: Beckham',
Euro 2004 Saturday 26 June 2004 available from
http://www.abc.net.au/sport/content/200406/
s1141011.htm, accessed 20 October, 2004

Adams, Alan. 'NHL Review', *Benchwarmer* Issue
102, available from http://www.benchwarmer.
co.uk/issue_archive/benchwarmer_issue_102.
pdf, accessed 27 May 2003

Baggio, Roberto. 'My Penalty Miss Cost Italy the
World Cup?' Sunday May 19, 2002, *The Observer*,

available from http://www.observer.co.uk/
Print/0,3858,4414765,00.html, accessed 30 May 2003

Chong, Jordan. 'All Eyes on McCartney', available from
http://kangaroosfc.com.au/default.asp?pg=news
&spg=display&articleid=97528, accessed 12 June 2003

Marche Region Tourism department. 'Marche Places:
Loreto' available from http://www.le-marche.com/
Marche/html/loreto.htm, accessed 22 December 2004

Matt Le Tiss. Com, available from http://www.
mattletiss.com/intro.php, accessed 28 December
2004

McWalter, Craig. 'Bill Shankly Quotes', available
from http://www.sportnetwork.net/main/s46/
st8936.htm, accessed 20 June 2003

Mitchell, John. 'ACT Soccer Federation Review of
Technical and Coaching Development in ACT
Soccer 2004', available from www.soccercanberra.
com.au, accessed 5 January 2005.

Moore, Leah. 'Soccer Mum's Red Card', available from
http://news.com.au/common/story_page/0,4057,
6723686%255E13762,00.html, accessed 11 July 2003

Nature, On-Line. 'Jackals of the African Crater',
available from http://www.pbs.org/wnet/
nature/jackals/index.html, accessed 13 July 2003

Patton, George S. 'Quotes' available from http://
www.brainyquote.com/quotes/authors/g/
george_s_patton.html, accessed 5 January 2005

Quayle, Emma. 'McCartney Seizes a Victory for the
Human Spirit', available from http://www.smh.
com.au/handheld/articles/2003/06/06/10547003
92986.htm, accessed 12 June 2003

Quotes Exchange, 'Soccer Quotes' available from

http://home.att.net/~quotesexchange/soccer.
html, accessed 13 July, 2003
Scott, Will. 'Tommy Docherty: Interviewed
February 2003', available from http://
www.newsshopper.co.uk/misc/print.
html?nwid=700214, accessed 20 May 2003

Articles

Banning, Jo. 'All I Know: Ric Charlesworth', *Inside Sport*, #138, July 2003

Bantick, Christopher. Australia's Forgotten Achievers', *The Canberra Times*, 30 December, 2004

Bond, Jeffrey. 'Training Willpower', *Sportscoach*, Vol. 26 No. 3, 2003

Conway, Doug. 'A Parent from Hell? Certainly not Mark's Dad', *The Canberra Times*, 5 July, 2003

Cooke, Graham. 'Win or lose, I love my team', *The Canberra Times*, 29 January, 2005

Coultan, Mark. 'Be A Sport and Keep a Lid On it', *Sydney Morning Herald*, June 15, 2004

FitzSimons, Peter. 'Great Motivational Speeches', *Sydney Morning Herald*, January 1, 2005

Hall, Matthew. 'Playing for Keeps', *Inside Sport*, #138, July 2003

Maddox, Gary, Mark. 'For Coaches, The Goals Go Way Beyond the Posts', *Sydney Morning Herald*, June 15, 2004

William Nack/Lester Munson/George Dohrmann.
'Out of Control', *Sports Illustrated*, 24 July 2000
Nicholson, Jamie. 'Football Improves Chance of
Death', *The Canberra Times*, 18 May 2003
'A Killer Punch', *The Canberra Times*, 1 July 2003
'Dad Attacked', *The Canberra Times*, 1 July 2003
'Waugh Plays Down Aggro', *The Canberra Times*, 18
May 2003

Song Lyrics

Joel, Billy, 'Pressure' from *The Nylon Curtain*
(Columbia), 1982.
Kiss, 'All Hell's Breaking Loose' from *Lick It Up*
(Mercury), 2003.
A Perfect Circle, '3 Libras' from *Mer de Noms*
(Virgin), 2000.
Pilot, 'Magic' from *Magic* (Disky), 1974.
Queen, 'We Are The Champions' from *News of the
World* (EMI), 1977.
Rage Against the Machine, 'Settle for Nothing' from
Rage Against the Machine (Sony), 1992.
REM, 'Losing My Religion' from *Out Of Time*
(Warner Bros), 2001.
The Who, 'Substitute' from *Meaty Beaty Big & Bouncy*
(MCA), 1966.

DVD

Bill Bryson's 'Notes from a Small Island': The Complete Television Series, Carlton International, 2002.

Hooligans & Thugs: Soccer's Most Violent Fan Fights, Narrated by Steve Jones 'The Original Punk Rocker', Umbrella Entertainment, 2004.

Michael Jordan : Come Fly With Me, Fox Video, 1989.

Loose reference was made in this book to the following films: *The Bad News Bears*, *A Beautiful Mind*, *Black Hawk Down*, *Biffs Bumps and Brawlers*, *Dodgeball*, *The Karate Kids* I–III, *The Mighty Ducks* I–III, *Mystery Alaska*, *Remember the Titans*, *Rocky* I–V, *Starship Troopers* and the original *Star Wars* trilogy.

Sorry, but there are lots of bad writers. Some are on-staff at your local newspaper, usually reviewing little theatre productions or pontificating about the local sports teams.

Stephen King, *On Writing*

17: Acknowledgements

I would like to thank the following teams who were informing and tolerating me at the time of writing:

The Radford Under 13 Div 1 & Under 17 Div 1 and Bill Turner Soccer squads of 2004; The Ladies' Men, Taipans, Black Thunder, Gunners and Vipers Under 12 Futsal sides; and the ACT Under 11 Colts (futsal). You all deserve a barnfull of jellysnakes.

I would also like to thank the following people who were cheering me on at the time of writing:

Nick Akhurst for capturing the moment
Barbara Coe for correcting the suspect action
Bruce Coe for checking the standings
Chris Conti for pulling the cards out
Paul and Virginia Dixon, Carl Allen and Sally Godtschalk and Sally Wodzinski for the Parents & Friends Association
Neil Hodgson for the Cascarino Technique
Sarah Kimball for pinch-hitting
Walter Learning and Jake Fraser for the live action-replay
Jann Lennard for disputes and disciplinary hearings

John and Val Leyshon for providing training
 facilities
Chris Lucas for stepping up
Stephen Matthews for organising the lamington
 drive
Stephen McIntyre for passing me some gems
Dylan Mordike for help with visualisation
David Mulford for putting the player into space
'Rufus' Wainwright for arguing game theory
Tom Wodzinski for accuracy in finish
And Mum for never dropping the ball in a tight
 situation.

Photographs in the middle bit were taken by the
rogue cameras of Nick Akhurst, Kaye Britten, Virginia
Dixon, Rory Kleeman, Dylan Mordike and Craig
Wainwright.

About the Author

George Huitker is a writer, coach and drama teacher entering his third decade at Radford College, Canberra. He has published three collections of poetry and two sporting memoirs, *Not Just Footy* (adapted for the stage in 2004 by Canadian director Walter Learning) and *How to Succeed Without Really Winning*, winner of an ACT Writing and Publishing Award in 2006.

He has formed various theatre companies and bands over the years, finally settling with his own independent theatre company, Huitker Movement Theatre (HMT) and his rock group, Junk Sculpture. In 2007, with Rachael Bishop, he founded teamSUPPORT, a project designed to encourage young people, particularly boys, to participate in charitable work.

George's website is at www.georgehuitker.com.au

Not Just Footy

George Huitker

It is refreshing to be reminded just what sport is all about. In the relaxed, insightful and entertaining style made famous by Bill Bryson, George Huitker recounts a lifetime of sporting experiences and anecdotes – delivering messages so often forgotten in these days of decreasing sports participation and increasing sports contracts.

Robert de Castella

Football is life and, as George Huitker says, not just footy. Huitker as a fan, a son of a fan, a player and a coach, narrates a classic every-man football story. The highs, the lows, the joys, the frustrations, the rewards and the ingratitude are all there in ways and doses we can recognise all too well. We have all played this game.

Les Murray

For George Huitker, footy is certainly not just footy. Coaching his kids allows George to express himself as a writer, and a teacher… George displays the kind of Australian passion and intensity for sport that must go a long way in explaining the incredible success this nation has enjoyed for many decades. His prose and poetry are sensitive, humorous and informative.

Dick Telford

277

I opened this book with trepidation... But by the end of the introduction I was excited. Here was passionate writing about sport as romance and fairy tale, that decried those who seek success at any cost and the commercialism of the game... Here is a writer who can unlock for me the mystery of why anyone has the slightest interest in sport... The book is a lovingly rendered meditation on a son's relationship with his father, as mediated by the game of soccer. It is a window into the strange world of school sporting competition. It edges towards being *Zen and the Art of Coaching a School's Sports Team*...

Not Just Footy is well worth a read, especially for a sports coach or a young player. Or a sports cynic.

Robin Davidson, *Muse*

George Huitker's book *Not Just Footy* allows our soccer community to celebrate its commitment and vitality. Outsiders can get some inkling of the human galaxies which revolve around that bouncing narcotic called, simply, 'ball'. The spirit of community, the conflict between success and ethics, the complacency of the winner, the desire of the loser. All of these emotions tumble out of Huitker's simple and special retelling of his experiences... In these days of inflated soccer industry egos and unimagined salaries, the people who matter are left behind. Huitker reminds us, sometimes hilariously, sometimes humiliatingly, but always with humility, of what it's really all about. His writing is part of the social cement which keeps us together. It puts things in context. It made me feel better. Buy it, read it, and you'll feel better too.

Danny Moulis

In the world of sport, published memoirs abound. Yet they are rarely worth reading. Such trips down memory lane usually deserve a flick through, but not close scrutiny... George Huitker's *Not Just Footy* is a shining exception to this trend. It is replete with questions about the socio-cultural significance of sport, reflections on the appropriate role of the coach, and criticisms against the idea that sporting acumen compensates for poor educational and social skills. His sense of what is possible moves from pessimism, to fatalism, and eventually to realism; that is, the players more so than the coach are responsible for their destiny. The coach, nonetheless, has a vital leadership role – not just by helping to develop sporting attributes, but also by promoting to young people valuable skills-for-life.

Dr Daryl Adair, *Sports Coach*

First-rate, original, distinguished by a congenial tone throughout. Includes an outstanding bibliography. If only we could all be so lucky as to have had George Huitker for a coach.

2006 ACT Writing & Publishing Awards Citation

If Bill Shankly's famous 'life and death' credo was about the destination, then Huitker's yarn is about the journey. The sequel to *Not Just Footy* continues the Canberra teacher, writer and football buff's coaching odyssey through the wild landscape of junior sport. It is one of the infinite intersections where stakeholders have the choice of embracing the inherent beauty and life-enforcing ways of the contest, or heading down the path to boorish beahviour and madness – a narrow tract between balance and obsession. Funny, tragic and richly sourced, it is not just a must-read for anyone like Uday Hussein, but all of us who've been temporarily unhinged by our sporting passions.

Neil Jameson – *Inside Sport*

The author's *leitmotiv* is that a win-at-all-costs attitude is positively harmful. As Huitker puts it, 'You can genuinely grow, develop and succeed through loss.' It seems to me that there is so much practical wisdom in this book that it should be required reading for all those involved in the vital task of coaching and supervising children's sport.

J. Neville Turner – *Sporting Traditions*

In *How To Succeed Without Really Winning* George Huitker has truly given us a gift. He has taken the time to reflect on our tendency to invest so much in the outcome of a 'measly game' of junior sport that the behaviour of adults – coaches, managers, parents and supporters – leaves much to be desired. This book should be required reading for everyone involved in junior sport, much the way that coaches are required to sign a Code of Ethics. A copy should be shared among the associates of every team! If the book is used as a guide, even once, it will have saved some juniors from the horrors most of us remember only too well.

Rae Wells – *Sports Coach*

Many sports, such as cricket, have – until recently, anyway – stressed that 'the game's the thing', and that the result should be secondary. But what's different about Huitker's book is its presentation, drawing on a frame of reference from Shakespeare to the Dalai Lama to lyrics from the pop group Kiss. In fact, in its gently didactic style, the book is reminiscent of Alain de Botton's *The Consolations of Philosophy* set in a sporting context.

Philip O'Brien – *The Canberra Times*

Little Life

George Huitker

'I loved Little Life... No doubt, our city has many stories of quiet service like this one. It is our loss that we do not hear more of them.' - Frank O'Shea, The Canberra Times

Turning 40, Huitker had the minor crisis that men are supposed to have at that age. He wondered whether teaching classes or directing actors around a stage or players around a football pitch was all he would do with his life. He describes the route that led him to set up teamSUPPORT, an outreach group among Year 10 boys at his school. Inspired by the book and film *Pay It Forward*, the boys – and now also the girls – organise and run activities with Black Mountain School and other organisations working with people with disabilities... I loved *Little Life*. The writing is fresh, the story uplifting... No doubt our city has many stories of quiet service like this one. It is our loss that we do not hear more of them.

Frank O'Shea – *The Canberra Times*

I read it within hours... *Little Life* showed me with clear-eyed objective attention to detail the terrible cost of dementia not only on George himself, but on all his relationships... In the face of suffering that marks human existence, we can take one of two paths: we can give in and give up, or we can take the experience and use it to transform the mess of our lives into something that lights the darkness. This is what *Little Life* does. It shows us vividly that all experience, no matter how harrowing and terrible, can be transfigured.

John Foulcher